2/17

Death Defied, Life Defined

A Miracle Man's Memoir

Paul E. Perkins
with Anita Agers Brooks

Clovercroft Publishing

Death Defied, Life Defined: A Miracle Man's Memoir

©2016 by Paul E. Perkins and Anita Agers Brooks

Independently published by the author through
Clovercroft Publishing, Franklin, Tennessee

Published in association with Larry Carpenter of
Christian Book Services, LLC of Franklin, Tennessee

Edited by Gail Fallen

Cover and Interior Design by Suzanne Lawing

Cover Watercolor by artist Doug Brega

ISBN: 978-1-942557-38-8

Printed in the United States of America

What People Are Saying About This Book

When someone dies and comes back to life a changed man, I listen. Paul Perkins is no longer afraid of what awaits him on the other side. His story of perseverance resurrects hope and will inspire you to savor each day to the max.

— CHERYL RICKER, *Co-author of* Rush of Heaven and Josiah's Fire

There's an old Cherokee saying that says, "You don't know who you are, until you know where you come from." Paul Perkins' story reminds us to ask ourselves the question, *Do you want to be right, or do you want to be renewed?* Then he takes us on a journey through *Death Defied, Life Defined,* that can help transform us by the renewing of our minds. After reading this true story, I am reminded again that we find our purpose when we follow our dreams, pursue our passions, and are champions for the good of others.

— DON CARLSON, *basketball coach and former MSU Bears player*

After meeting Paul, and hearing about his challenges with his health I was fascinated to hear his story. Just the fact that he has survived death more than once, and is living to tell the story would be motion picture worthy! The miracles continue when he gets to meet the family of the brave young man who gave up his organs for others to live. This memoir is truly a testimony of survival against all odds. Paul's faith and dedication to his family and The Lord plays the biggest role in his life. I know that anyone who reads this book will become a better person because of Paul and Linda's example of resilience — they never give up. I'm grateful to have this family as my friends and encourage all to read this book.

    — LILY ISAACS, *Country and bluegrass gospel music group The Isaacs*

Death Defied, Life Defined is one of the most inspirational books I have come across in a very long time. A story of loss and sorrow mirrored by joy and redemption. This true account of a man who nearly lost his life and discovered God in the center of it all, teaches us what living truly means. Paul's dramatic tale is not only intriguing, but shines clarity on the issues of life and death.

    — DARREN DAKE, *author of* Unrighteous: A Story of One Man's Road to Redemption

I have had the privilege of knowing Paul for the last few years. The first thing I noticed about him was his generosity and passion for life. This was before I knew of the battle he fought for his life. *Death Defied, Life Defined* is a look into Paul's heart. He invites readers to join him as he goes through his greatest victories and most crushing defeats. I can attest to the fact that a person cannot come into contact with Paul and not have their passion for life reignited. In this book, his words become his presence and by the end your passion for life will be reignited.

    — JOSH LINDBLOM, *Professional Baseball Player*

Paul's story about his life and everything he overcame is truly amazing. More importantly, it reminds us how fragile we are and what is truly important in our lives. I found the book to be well written and inspiring.

— DONALD D. HUTSTON, JR., *CPA, National Financial Services Partner*

My wife, Diana, and I have known Paul Perkins' and his family for many years through business relationships that became a firm friendship. I knew him first in my role as editor-in-chief of *BankNews* magazine, when it became apparent he was a respected Missouri banker known for his passion for his community and for community banking. Later, Diana, as an account executive with Unico Group Inc., worked with him on analyzing and serving his bank's insurance needs. We grew to admire him as a businessman of integrity, honesty and strong character, and a nurturing father and husband. We were stunned at the news of his extremely serious health issues, and relieved at his remarkable recovery. That he lived to recount in this book his perilous journey of the past few years is a blessing that should inspire all of us to never give up in the face of adversity, no matter how dire.

— BILL POQUETTE, *Editor-in-Chief, BankNews Media*

Mayo Clinic considers it an honor and a privilege to have a role in the care of each and every patient we serve. Mayo Clinic's Mission: "To inspire hope and contribute to health and well-being by providing the best care to every patient through integrated clinical practice, education, and research." Our first consideration is always that the needs of the patient come first.

— DAVID L. HAYES, MD

Paul Perkins' *Death Defied, Life Defined* is a chronicle and journey from here to the after-life and back. For me, a journey set-forth in a personal narrative from a best friend. A narrative that imparts an unvarnished understanding of what tomorrow may bring. While reading chapter by chapter, I could not wait to continue reading to discover what the next chapter would say. To me, this amazing true life story gives clear insight about the after-life.

— JAMES C. SHIELDS, *CEO and Managing Partner, J. Crawford Associates, Inc.*

As someone who lived these events with Paul and Linda Perkins over the years, *Death Defied, Life Defined* is such a reminder of all that God did for them through Paul's illness. I am so excited to see how this book will used for God's glory and to help others through their struggles. I appreciate being part of their mission to share Christ's love, hope, and grace.

— BECKY SIMPSON, *Marketing Director, First Community National Bank*

Perkins shares with us a frank and fundamentally optimistic exploration of his fight to regain his health and places that struggle in the context of his strong faith. Everyone can find something to feel good about in this story.

— LARRY K. HARRIS, *Polsinelli PC, Polsinelli LLP in California*

An amazing recount of a life interrupted by crisis and redeemed by grace. A testimony to God's faithful provision and unconditional love. Reading this memoir will both challenge and inspire those facing difficult days, revealing the healing power and intrinsic value of writing the stories that matter most. A message worthy of your time.

— KAREN JORDAN, *author of* Words That Change Everything

Dedication

This book is dedicated to my beautiful bride of forty-six years, Linda. Without you, I am half a man. Because of you, I am complete.

To my children, Mark, Scott, and Julie, a father couldn't be more proud than I am of you.

To my grandchildren, your Papa is so blessed that God chose to let me love you.

To my brothers, John and Joe, without your encouragement and love, I would have encountered a much steeper mountain to climb.

To my family at First Community National Bank, thank you for your support, dedication, and care.

To my friends, who prove repeatedly that strong men and women are held up by powerful prayer and caring hands.

To the medical teams who attended me, my gratitude runs as deep, wide, and long, as the mighty Mississippi running through my home state.

To all of the coaches who shaped me into a man of discipline, your teaching probably helped save my life.

And to Don Carlson, a true friend, a man with whom I have much in common, and whose "two thumbs up" attitude is displayed today on the MSU Basketball Bears uniforms. You were the perfect Champion and Fighter, but understood when the contest was over. Like the true warrior you were, Sportsmanship and Character graced your life to the end. I am honored to call you friend. I love and miss you.

Foreword

When I entered the room at Rochester's Mayo Clinic in April of 2014, I was surprised to see Paul's grin, offered from a sitting position. I expected a weaker greeting, from a man confined to his hospital bed.

"You made it," Paul welcomed me with enthusiasm.

After having undergone a double transplant surgery only a couple of weeks prior — one giving him a new kidney, the other a new heart — I thought he looked good. I hugged his wife, Linda, and sat in the chair next to her, across from Paul.

It didn't take long for him to repeat something he'd told me three months earlier — before he received his new organs. "I want you to write my story. I think a lot of people could benefit from hearing about what I've been through."

I chuckled, "Okay, when you're stronger we'll talk about it."

Paul repeated his request. "I'm serious. I told you before, I want you to write my book."

"How about if you focus on letting your body heal right now, and when you get home to Missouri, we'll schedule a time to discuss it."

Paul nodded his head in agreement with a hint of laughter in his voice. Then, he explained his determined resolve to record his story as soon as possible. "I don't want to wait too long. I'm not sure how much time I have."

Those words got my attention — I knew from my own transplant experience, Paul spoke the truth.

I nearly died in 1997, after a severe allergic reaction to my pain meds post-transplant. The surgery itself went perfectly. But my medical crisis proved to me the importance of being prepared for the future, especially for eternity. You never know what might end your life — or when.

At the time, I didn't realize my experience would transform my life in amazing ways, or that God would use it to help others. Nor did I foresee the privilege of sharing another organ transplant story. But Paul's experience inspired me.

I gave an organ to my sister, while Paul is a double recipient from a young man he never met named Cooper. Though are roles in transplant differ, I discovered many similarities in mine and Paul's stories. We both observed things few others will see before they leave this earth.

This is why Paul's narrative especially intrigued me. We both witnessed the curtain drawn back and glimpsed the spiritual world beyond earth. Peering past the thin veil of death, we discovered a renewed hope for eternity.

When I came close to death, it drew me to God. It awakened me to the fragility of life, and exposed my misaligned priorities. When I stood at the threshold of eternity, I resolved never to let some things happen again, given a second chance.

Paul's epiphany strikes a brutal chord of reality. God is not a distant acquaintance you pick up or discard when you are in the mood, or when a situation makes Him convenient. Instead, God is the Master of the Universe — someone to cherish, honor, and obey at all times, not just during a crisis.

Many people will relate to Paul's story, whether they enjoy exceptional health or struggle to survive — whether they fear death or welcome Heaven as their true home. No matter how strong we think we are, nothing communicates the truth of our humanity like preparing to face our Maker. But as Paul reminds us, when we know Jesus, death loses its sting. And the best is yet to come.

—*Anita Agers Brooks*
    inspirational business/life coach, international speaker, and
    award-winning author of *Getting Through What You Can't Get
    Over*, Barbour Publishing, 2015

Preface

What does it feel like to die?

I expected the final breaths of my life to feel different. To look different — how little I had thought about the end. Prior to my own death, I didn't allow myself to focus on conjecture. I didn't want to waste my life obsessing over my death.

However, there were some after-life things I wondered about at times.

- *Are Heaven and Hell real places?*
- *Do we instantly wake up on the other side when we die, or do we sleep in the grave waiting for the big wake-up call?*
- *Is the dying process slow, or is the light of life snuffed out in a blink?*
- *Will we feel panic or peace as we slip into the realm of the eternal unknown?*
- *Is there truly something beautiful waiting across a distant shore?*

My questions were answered, and then confirmed a second time. Most people die once, leaving loved ones to mourn and wonder what it's like crossing from one world to another. Because of my experiences, I know what to expect when I pass a final time. My doctor confirmed that I died at least twice . . . and added, "Probably more."

If you have lost someone you loved or if you fear dying, I hope my story helps, because death is not the end. For many of us, the best is yet to come.

CHAPTER ONE

Miracle Man

The voice on the other end got straight to the point. "Are you with your mom and dad?"

"Sort of. We're at the Mall of America, but we're separated right now. I can find them though."

"I'm with the transplant team at Mayo, and I think we have a heart for your dad."

My grown daughter, Julie, squealed out loud in the mall, "You what?"

"But you have to be here by 7:00, not a minute later."

Julie looked at her watch, it was just after 5:00 — she knew the drive to Rochester would take an hour and a half under normal driving conditions. Plus, we were all separated in the largest mall in the United States. There was not a second to waste.

***

Julie almost didn't receive the call telling us a new heart and kidney were waiting for me on March 16, 2014 — but more about that later.

Throughout the years preceding my double transplant, while disease ravaged my body and anguish plagued my mind, I brushed against the curtain of death on multiple occasions. Many in the medical community told me, "You are truly a miracle man. You should not be alive."

I survived when death seemed certain — for a purpose. You are part of my destiny. You are included in God's plan. I believe my story will inspire you to live fully in who you were created to be. My question to you is this, "Will you dare believe you were made for more?"

In the early hours of March 17, 2014, I received a new heart and a new kidney. These priceless gifts came from a twenty-year-old young man whose compassion and care for others propelled his family to continue his legacy — by their decision to donate his organs. I'll tell you about these amazing people as my story progresses.

While you read, I trust you'll see my passion for legacy. I want to leave an inheritance of hope — for my family, my friends, and you. Through my experience I learned lessons, discovered renewed joy, and uncovered secrets. But I don't want to keep them to myself. For now, however, let's get back to my story.

My transplant surgery took place at the Mayo Clinic in Rochester, Minnesota, where I experienced an other-worldly encounter. Prior to my organ transplants, I died twice in St. Louis, as confirmed by my physicians.

I'm sure there are variances in the dying process, depending on circumstances just prior to the final breath. But I know without a doubt, what it feels like to pass on. And let me assure you, there are surprises waiting on the other side.

My multiple encounters with death shouldn't cause astonishment — I rarely do anything the normal way. When all appears lost, I know from experience, a greater plan is at work. It seems my life is scripted by Divine fingers.

Like George Bailey, from the classic movie, *It's a Wonderful Life*, I have been given a second chance. However, I did not know about George or our parallels, until recently.

I can't say how I lived sixty-six years without seeing it. I missed something many embraced for decades. Yet, less than nine months after doctors at the Mayo Clinic placed a new heart and kidney into my body, I finally sat down with my wife, Linda, and watched *It's a Wonderful Life*.

Though not mirror images, it didn't take long for me to see the similarities between myself and George. We both had hard working parents who embodied honesty, faith, and integrity. We both have military champions for brothers. And we are both bankers, dedicated to doing our part for the greater good of our communities and the people who comprise them — sometimes sacrificing self to get the job done. I don't say this to brag, because frankly it humbles me that I've been blessed by so many. I offer you a deeper understanding by the dramatic events of my story. I have truly lived a wonderful life — but by human standards, I shouldn't be here to share the details.

I grew up as the youngest of three sons. My brothers are smart, handsome, and funny. They are also my heroes. Joe the oldest, and ten years my senior, is a gifted leader. When he sees a problem, he immediately determines a solution and takes charge to implement it. I think his placement in our birth order, plus his training and experience serving in the Army as an officer at the height of the Vietnam conflict, charted him for greatness.

John, three and a half years older than me, also fought and led great fighting men in Vietnam. As the middle son, he exemplifies diplomacy, wisdom, and discretion. I'm sure these qualities are why he was promoted to high ranking positions within some of our nation's most powerful and protective agencies.

Because of men like Joe and John, we breathe the fresh air of freedom here in the United States of America.

I admire both of my brothers for their pivotal guidance in my life. Like George Bailey, I wouldn't be who I am today if it weren't for these relationships God provided.

I am deeply grateful for the ones who came before me — my brothers, parents, grandparents, and extended family members. As you'll soon learn, not only did they shape my life, they also paved many beautiful and life-altering paths for others in the regions they founded and helped maintain. Some brought their traditions from a land far across ocean waves, overcoming adversity, leaving a mark of tenacity. The invincible spirit of my ancestors flows through my veins. It is most likely the reason I am alive to tell you what happened, and how the events of my stories might impact you.

I am also thankful for my beautiful children and grand-children. But my deepest indebtedness goes to my wife, who walks by my side. Maybe that's why it surprised me that my family wasn't a concern as I entered Heaven — when I died the first time. My experience was short, sweet, and very surprising.

When I left my body, the transition was peace-filled and comforting beyond anything I've felt before or since. My spirit immediately entered the supernatural world. There were no white or bright lights. There was no sensation of moments passing. In less time than it takes to blink an eye, I stood in the presence of people who had already died. My thoughts swirled with emotion, but nothing I sensed matched what I would have anticipated.

As much as I treasure my wife, two sons, daughter, and grandchildren, I would have expected my heart to ache. After all, I had abandoned them as I departed life on earth. They are normally in my thoughts, but they weren't the focus after my death. Instead, my thoughts were focused on where I was and what I was seeing.

In that heavenly place, I stood in the presence of people whose sweet faces consumed my attention. I looked into the eyes of loved ones I hadn't thought about in a very long time — people who influenced my life. Gaps in my memory were suddenly filled with renewed love. Our reunion brought complete restoration.

I could feel Christ around, in, and through everything and everyone. From the instant I arrived, all pain was left in the past. Happiness like I'd never known flooded me.

I had made it home — one of the miracles is my ability to tell you the story.

ACTS 17:26 (HCSB)
"From one man He has made every nationality to live over the whole earth and has determined their appointed times and the boundaries of where they live."

CHAPTER TWO

My Second After-Life

If I had imagined my last breaths, I might have envisioned a long tunnel immersed in a white light — but this was not part of my experience.

Just before passing in Rochester, Minnesota, I realized I was seeing square lights, of many different colors. Some of the squares were filled in, some were not. Red, yellow, orange, green, and white — they surrounded me and seemed to bob and weave around my head. They were brighter than anything I had seen before. Fluorescent tubes, but somehow connected. At first, I thought it would never stop. But then things changed.

Though slight, I felt fear. I was experiencing something new. I was afraid of what I was facing. I could see the operating room. I was part of the scene, yet a disconnected observer — somehow, at the same time. At first, I remained in my bed, looking up.

Two doctors were working on me. One shook his head saying, "He's not going to make it."

I saw him turn to one of the nurses. "You can disconnect him and move him when you're ready."

I thought to myself, *I'm not going to die.*

Two of the nurses were talking while they removed a couple of tubes from my still body.

I asked, "Why are you taking those tubes out?"

They ignored me and continued talking to each other. This really aggravated me, so I tried again. "Hey, I'm still alive you know."

They continued their conversation, as if I had remained silent. The entire time, they bustled around disconnecting equipment, thinking I was already dead.

After a while, one of them said, "Let's take a break and grab a cup of coffee."

Apparently they did this nearby, because I could still hear their chatter — as if I was at the table with them. I heard everything they said.

One of the nurses said, "Can you believe she's having an affair with her husband?"

The other nurse replied, "You know cops are notorious for sleeping around. You couldn't pay me to marry a police officer."

"I don't care what he does, there's no excuse for cheating with his wife's friend. Except, no real friend would do that either. They're both scum if you ask me."

The entire time they gossiped, I felt uncomfortable and awkward that they would discuss the affair while I was there. I wanted them to stop.

I kept waiting for them to discover their mistake. Surely they would soon realize what they were doing. But that's not what happened.

When they finally returned to the operating suite, one of the nurses said, "He's gone."

This stirred me up, and I attempted to correct her. "I am

not gone. I'm here."

But, the nurse who'd spoken left.

The other nurse stayed, watching the monitors and putting away instruments. Finally she disconnected me from the last machine. Then everything shifted, I was no longer looking up from my bed. Instead, I was viewing the entire room from above.

Her nursing friend returned and said, "He's unhooked now."

I tried again, "I'm not gone, I'm right here."

"I'll call Carl to come get him."

"No, please don't do this," I cried.

A few minutes later, an orderly wheeled in a long wooden box.

I protested. "Please don't put me in that."

But they didn't respond. Instead, they folded the sides down to open up the box, lifted my body from the gurney. Suddenly, my frame of reference changed again as the two box sides folded above my body. I was inside a dark, enclosed space. I had now returned to my body.

I beat on the box lid, trying to get someone to hear me. "Let me out. I'm not dead. I'm not dead."

They shuttled me down to the basement and parked me in a cold, silent room.

Through this whole experience, I was aware of a raging thunderstorm. Great bolts of lightening struck the ground nearby, followed by massive booms of rolling thunder. Not only did I see and hear the strikes, but I felt tremors when a couple of them penetrated the ground.

A short time later, two men placed me in a black Chevrolet Suburban. As thick pellets of rain pounded my box, I pounded and screamed from inside.

In an instant, I was freed from the box. Unfettered by the constraints of my flesh, watching the reactions of others.

In a hospital waiting room, a doctor was telling my family I was gone.

Everyone was crying, except Mark, my oldest child, who stood strong. He hugged my wife and said, "Mom, I'm going to take a flight out now, so I can go home and tell people in person, instead of them getting the bad news on social media. I'll let them know how hard he fought, but that he lost the final battle. I'll start making arrangements like Dad would want."

Linda, my beautiful and faithful wife, nodded, sobbing on his chest a few more minutes before he left.

As I watched, my only sadness was for my family, mingled with pride about Mark's maturity. I didn't feel sorry for myself; I experienced no pain, I simply wanted my loved ones to know how peaceful I felt — but I realized it was no longer possible for me to communicate.

Again, space and time evaporated. I could see how Mark and my two other children, Scott and Julie, were keeping their promises to honor me in a fitting way.

My spent body was positioned on the basketball court in our hometown Steelville Middle School. The gym was crammed with people sitting on the bleachers and lined around the court perimeter. I saw my family of course, along with other familiar faces, including fellow church members. Some mourners were banking clients. I'd served with many attendees on community projects.

I had always joked that they should bury me under the basketball court, because that's where I'd spent much of my life. It was the perfect choice for a final farewell.

Pastor Jerry Beers preached my funeral service, along with a couple of eulogies given by close friends. As I listened, I was not sad and I shed no tears. I felt no heaviness of body — it was as if I was lighter than air, floating without effort. I had never known such sheer joy before. And then, it ended.

The next thing I knew, I opened my eyes in a hospital room.

I was back in my body, alive.

What I experienced wasn't a dream. What happened to me in that operating room through my funeral service was vivid. This other world — call it a parallel universe, simultaneous happening, another dimension, or a premonition — was real. I actually attended my own funeral.

This outlines those events I experienced the second time I died. Previously, when illness attacked my body in St. Louis, I first encountered death and the afterlife. But when I came back the first time, I didn't tell anyone about it. I lacked the courage. When I first became sick, I couldn't have known how much my life would change post-transplant and post-survival. I am not the same man who entered the Mayo Clinic.

Before my illness, I was strong, independent, and confident. But with a few changes in my body, and one devastating diagnosis, I learned how fragile life really is — and how quickly one's fortune can change. I learned what it's like to walk through the valley of death.

1 CORINTHIANS 15:55 (NIV)
"Where, O death, is your victory?
Where, O death, is your sting?"

CHAPTER THREE

Pain Is Not Always a Gain

In my younger years, I played basketball competitively, achieving high success at the college level. My 6'4" height and wiry body type helped me move the ball away from defenders and into the hoop.

When you're an athlete, as I was most of my life, you get used to pushing through aches and strains. But for someone who's sick, pain can signal a coming game-changing event.

My high tolerance for pain helped me excel in sports. Coupled with my over-achieving mindset, this explains why I didn't respond to my illness sooner. With years of conditioning behind me, when something hurt, I kept going.

In my youth, it served me well. I learned to tune out my body when discomfort hit.

At age thirty-one, the Army Reserve doctor discharging me asked a surprising question. He was older, and straightforward. "Captain Perkins, have you experienced any wooziness lately?"

"Not really," I said.

He scratched his head. "You've got a little something going on. I recommend you see a specialist for your heart."

I was perplexed, but not alarmed. As I thought about it, I remembered several times when I was light-headed and had unusual feelings in my chest.

Without the Army's requirement for an exit physical before releasing me from their reserve program, I wouldn't have known about my heart defect. I didn't notice the early symptoms, so I wouldn't have sought treatment until much later — maybe after it was too late.

I now know how important it is to pay attention to your body, and respond quickly to anything that signals change.

Within days, I was scheduled for a stress test at Barnes-Jewish Hospital in St. Louis, near my hometown of Steelville, Missouri. The physician reviewed the results, then ordered an echocardiogram. An echocardiogram uses sound waves to produce images of your heart. It allows physicians to see the human heart beating and pumping blood, enabling them to identify disease.

Afterward, the physician called me into his office and said, "I see from your medical history that your mother died young from heart disease. In her late sixties. Is that right?"

"Yes," I recalled somberly.

"This is nothing to be alarmed about, you're in the preliminary stages, but you have a hereditary heart disease called Hypertrophic Cardiomyopathy."

"Is it bad?"

"This condition is usually caused by gene mutations that cause the heart muscle to grow abnormally thick. Your echo shows thickness causing hardness in the muscle, creating what we call a stiff heart. People with hypertrophic cardiomyopathy also have an abnormal arrangement of heart muscle cells, a condition known as myofiber disarray. This disarray can contribute to arrhythmia in some people."

"I don't understand, I get plenty of exercise, and I eat pretty good."

"The form of heart disease you have is usually inherited, and with your mother's early passing, I'm guessing she passed it on to you. There's a 50 percent chance that the children of a parent with hypertrophic cardiomyopathy will inherit the genetic mutation for the disease. Close relatives — parents, children, or siblings are at risk.

In simple terms, your heart is overworked on one side, while the other side beats at a normal rate. The pressure isn't balanced, and it prevents blood from properly feeding your brain. Your disease isn't caused by anything you've done, it's just the cards you were dealt."

"Is there a cure?"

"You'll need to take precautions, and I want to put you on medication. I'll want to see you every couple of years so I can monitor your progress and watch for any changes. We'll evaluate as we go."

The doctor's confident tone and treatment outline eased any concerns I might have had. *He's got it under control,* I thought.

For a time I lived normally, only giving my condition a passing thought as I took my daily meds, or when it was time for me to see the specialist in St. Louis. But eventually, things changed. My competitive nature rang the first warning bell.

I noticed how often my wife, Linda, beat me at checkers and card games. This was not the norm. In the beginning, I laughed with her, as she reveled in victory. "I win again," she'd say with delight.

But soon, I realized this was a permanent change. It was obvious my wife agreed, as her laughter turned to concern. "Is something wrong?"

"I'm not sure," I answered honestly.

I started paying closer attention to other mental habits. It was harder for me to process thoughts like I used to. I became frustrated.

Why couldn't I think clearly?

Where did my strategic planning abilities go?

Even though the doctor had clearly communicated the details of my heart condition, including the improper blood flow to my brain, I didn't attribute hypertrophic cardiomyopathy as a connection to my muddled mind.

I concluded old-age forgetfulness must be setting in, though forty-something was far too young for that. But it made more sense than anything else I considered — connecting it to my heart condition didn't occur to me.

Another clue came on the basketball court. I still played in a recreational league, and suddenly, I began to have a harder time keeping up. My energy was flagging, and my muscles were becoming unusually sore. At first, I did what I'd always done — pushed through.

No pain, no gain, I told myself, but the outcome wasn't the same as in the past. I couldn't play harder. I couldn't deaden the fatigue and body aches. It saddened me to hang up my basketball shoes, but my body and mind knew it was time.

Once I gave up the intensity of basketball, and let myself recuperate, I seemed to bounce back — for a few years. I needed something to replace the sport I'd sorrowfully sacrificed, so I took up the less intensive game of golf.

Physically, I did fine, but mentally and emotionally, I struggled. I preferred playing a team sport, not one where you can only blame yourself when the game doesn't turn out well. I wanted to master it, but that didn't happen.

In 2001, when I was in my early 50's, my doctor alerted me to a change. After so many years, we were more than just a patient and doctor — we were close friends. I trusted him with my life.

"The echo doesn't really show anything distressing," he

said, "but there's something different from the previous ones you've had. It's more a feeling I have than something I can point to on a report," he explained.

Dr. Jerry Dwyer ran his finger down a piece of paper, as if looking for information. He talked while he searched. "I'm going to send you for a CT Scan. I think it might tell me more."

I had the procedure and was back in his office within a few days.

Jerry didn't waste any time telling me the results. "You have an aneurysm next to your aortic artery. If it grows large enough, it can kill you instantly. We need to remove it as soon as possible. I want to refer you to Dr. Mauney."

I wasn't going to argue.

Dr. Michael Mauney, a cardiac surgeon, did not toy with his words. "You are at a six," he said. "We judge by size, and six centimeters is a benchmark number. An aneurysm often bursts between six and a half and seven centimeters. I want to see you in three months, then I can measure this bulge and determine whether it's growing, or if this is something you've always had and your body is adjusted to it."

I admit I felt mildly stunned knowing my body could implode at any given moment. A half a centimeter didn't seem like much wiggle room.

Three months later, after another scan, he gave me the results. "There's been some growth. We can't wait. We need to get you into surgery right away."

I entered the hospital in January, 2002, and was prepped for the procedure. This would be the first time I'd ever gone under a scalpel.

Dr. Mauney visited my room to tell me what to expect. But he had more to discuss than the removal of my aneurysm. "I'm going to talk to you in midwestern layman's terms," he said.

"Okay."

"When I'm in there for your aortic root replacement, I should do a Septal myectomy, where I fillet some of that hard muscle off your heart, so it isn't so stiff. Do you understand why we need to do this?"

His choice of words stunned me, and I envisioned all kinds of images. As a fisherman, I understood exactly what he meant by using the word, "fillet." But after my mind relaxed, I knew how to respond.

"Let me ask you a question, if I was your dad, what would you do? Would you fillet it out?"

"Yes, I would."

"Then do it."

I had all night to think about the operation, and the possibility of death, before they came for me in the early hours of the next morning. Fearful thoughts ran through my head. I'd never seriously considered my own mortality before. I knew I would die someday, but thinking about when and how was not something I'd given myself permission to explore. However, now I had no choice. There was a better than average possibility I might not survive the procedure.

Years before the operation, I read the Bible, accepted Jesus Christ as my Savior, and was baptized. I raised my children in church, as my parents had raised me. But I confess to you, Jesus was not first in importance to me then.

The order of my priorities was family, self, and career.

Today, my priority is putting my faith in Jesus into action — spreading the good word about God's love, caring for my family, and helping others.

My health complications re-set my priorities. It started in my bed, while I contemplated what might happen to me during the two pending surgical procedures — one to remove a dangerous aneurysm, and one to remove the layers of thickened muscle from my weakened heart.

I asked myself, *What have I done wrong in life? Who have I treated badly? Am I truly right with God?*

After making a mental list of my sins, I confessed them to Jesus and thanked him for dying on the cross so I could be forgiven. As I lay there contemplating my life, I realized I knew *about* Jesus from attending church most of my life, but I couldn't say we had a personal relationship. We weren't close, and it was my fault. I couldn't risk eternity hoping I *might* be okay with the one who sacrificed his life to save mine.

Because I had read the Bible, and through experience had come to trust the truth of its wisdom, I knew Jesus is the only way, the only truth, and the only pathway to eternal life. But my actions did not mirror those beliefs.

Facing the possibility of death made me realize many things. While medical machines whirred around me, I tossed under crisp, sterilized hospital sheets, alone in a darkened room with God, as my thoughts churned non-stop.

A committed athlete would not go into a ballgame with the kind of apathy I'd treated my Christian faith with, so why had I treated Jesus so carelessly?

What if Revelation 3:16 was right, and my lukewarm commitment to Christ caused Him to spew me out of His mouth?

Why was I afraid to publicly show my love and appreciation for someone who demonstrated His love by dying for me?

A chill caused my body to tremor from toe to head. Then I thought about my blessings.

Why was I given a great family and a good life?

Where had I displayed my gratitude to God?

What gifts had I given back?

Who had I touched in a positive way?

If provided the opportunity, I decided to spend the rest of my life giving more and taking less for granted. In my hospital bed, I prayed.

Jesus,

I'm sorry for sitting on the bench, when you called me to get out there and give you my all. Please forgive me. If I have more time, I want to make a real difference. I want to contribute. I want to show you my gratitude. But I can't do it on my own. I don't have the strength or the know-how. I realize I need a lot of coaching, but I trust you to guide me. And I promise to be teachable. I'll listen, and I'll do what you tell me. Thank you for dying on the cross for me. I don't deserve you, but I appreciate you. Thank you for being my Savior. I give myself to you, however long I have left on Earth.

Amen

As I was finishing, a nurse came in. In her matter-of-fact-manner, she said, "Mr. Perkins, I'm here to scrub you down."

My body froze. No woman had ever scrubbed me before. I couldn't imagine anyone but my wife seeing my naked body. I'm sure the look on my face resembled a cat's — just before being plunged into a tub of water.

But acting like she didn't have a care in the world, my nurse went about the business of washing me from head to toe. I was mortified. She smiled, and I realized she really enjoyed her job — a little too much for me.

After she left, still smiling, I lay very still listening to the beeps tracking my vitals. Once I got used to their peculiar noises, I went back to my reflective thoughts. I couldn't sleep.

Before the coral pink sun had peeked fully across the ebony horizon, my room filled with concerned people. My wife, two sons, and daughter, along with Pastor Jerry Beers, from a local church back home, came to see me. They comforted me and Jerry prayed. He walked alongside the gurney as the medical staff rolled me down the hall to the operating suite.

It was the first time in my life I'd been on the receiving end of a prayer spoken aloud. I'd asked God to help others, but I'd not really needed help myself. Before this, if there was a problem, I figured out a solution, and went about the business of doing something about it. But this one I couldn't fix alone.

Jerry knew. My family knew. I knew. Only God could guide the hands of the doctors and give them wisdom. Only God would decide if I lived or died. Only God knew if I would open my eyes on this side of Heaven again.

I don't know how long the surgery lasted, or how much time passed before I came out of the fog of anesthesia. But when I realized I'd survived, I was ecstatic. The surgery had gone well.

Dr. Mauney removed the aneurysm, and ran a line through the valve area. However, the surgeon discovered the bulge was bigger than they thought and had left permanent damage in its wake. He had no choice but to sew a new tube on my aortic, and insert a metal valve. Because of my new hardware, I would now have to take Warfarin, the generic equivalent of Coumadin, to keep my blood thin to reduce the risk of clotting.

As an active outdoorsman, it was a blow and a setback to my quality of life. I couldn't take things for granted as I had in the past.

I'd have to exercise extreme caution, because even a tiny cut while taking this powerful blood thinner could make me bleed profusely. If I bumped my head hauling hay, it could spur massive blood flow. Any small tear inside my body could cause internal seepage without my realizing it. A bleeding ulcer could make me hemorrhage to death. It changed how I would live the rest of my days.

I realized pain is not always a gain. Yes, I was breathing, but could I enjoy the time I was given? Could I keep my promises to God? I wanted to think yes.

Over time, as I regained my strength, my old optimism returned with it. Maybe a bit too much.

I didn't strictly follow the advice from any of my doctors, and so I decided against out-patient occupational therapy. I thought I could do it on my own. That was a mistake. I learned in a dangerous way, there's a balancing act between positive thinking and realistic precautions.

Because I didn't adhere to the doctor's instructions, I never did reach optimal health for my age. My home therapy was not as beneficial as professionals in their facilities could have provided. I regret that decision today.

Reflecting back, not following doctors' orders was not the only mistake I made. During this period, I relied on myself instead of listening to the experts, and I did the same with God.

Once I recovered, I took life and healing for granted. I expected God to fix me, so I didn't thank Him like I should have.

I often wonder now:

How many times did He protect me when I wasn't paying attention?

How many golf balls missed my head, keeping me from bleeding to death?

How many car accidents did He help me avoid?

How many tripping hazards did He remove from my path?

Though I didn't express my gratitude at that time, it didn't mean I wasn't thankful. I just didn't come to the point where I regularly told God I appreciated Him, saying, "Thank you," for all He had done.

Instead, when I regained my strength, I resumed my life thinking I would do what I'd done in my past — I would push through to a better outcome. I hadn't yet learned how to listen and rely on Jesus.

I thought I could still manage my life on my own terms, in my own power and strategy, barreling through when necessary. I thought mentally quoting, *No pain, no gain,* was enough. Except, as I would discover repeatedly, pain does not always produce a gain — and without Jesus, no human effort is enough.

The lesson hadn't soaked in — obviously I needed to retake the test again and again, until I could finally pass. But instead of getting easier, each one was harder than the last. Yet I refused to give up.

No matter the difficulty, failure is not in my vocabulary; it's not in God's either. That's why I can share with you what happened next.

HEBREWS 12:11 (NIV)

"No discipline seems pleasant at the time, but painful. Later on, however, it produces a harvest of righteousness and peace for those who have been trained by it."

CHAPTER FOUR

Free Thinkers and Odd Fellows

For a few years, I became accustomed to the new me. I had to make changes, and though I didn't feel as good as I had before my heart problems surfaced, I adjusted. Often, I didn't notice how bad I felt, as I pushed ahead, determined to live productively. But I quickly learned, no matter what my mindset, there were some things I could not control. Chronic, genetic health issues was one of them.

Stepping off the plane felt like stepping out of a time machine, where my twenty-first century present met my family's past. The landscape was mesmerizing, rich in cultural history. It was 2009, and we had flown into Prague — far from the comfort of home. Shortly after arriving at the hotel, I cut myself shaving, and the blood thinner did its work.

Immediately, I began to bleed profusely, and I wondered if I would hemorrhage to death in a foreign land. Though Prague is the fifteenth largest city in the European Union, and the historical capital of Bohemia as part of the Czech Republic, I still didn't want to test their modern medical practices. Thankfully,

I stopped the blood flow without having to go to a hospital.

I couldn't help wondering if this trip was worth it, even as much as I'd really wanted to travel. Between the intensity of the bleeding and my reduced energy level — I was wiped out. But I didn't say anything, not wanting to ruin things for my family.

Linda and I were in Europe with my brother, Joe, and his wife, Laurie. Our mission was to visit the place of our Bohemian roots. I proudly carry the Perkins name, but the Baloun influence from my mom's side of the family is no less a part of who I am.

We rented a car and driver in Prague, and drove to Klatovy, 135km away, where the Baloun extension of our family line lived in the eighteen-hundreds. Situated in the Plzen region of Western Bohemia near the German border, Klatovy's history dates back to at least 1263 A.D.

Entering the city, the skyline of Klatovy is replete with modern sculptures and old bastions — linking present and past Baroque architecture. Klatovy's red tiled roofs cover elegant buildings surrounded by the Sumava Mountains, and is famous for traditional goods, historic sights, and flowering carnations cultivated from tiny blossoms that originated from France. It is an exquisite sight to see.

As I touched the hallowed land of my mother's familial roots, I was determined to find the remains of those who had trod before me. We began our quest in an ancient cemetery, just as an intense thunderstorm struck.

Lightning blazed the sky in unrelenting bursts while sheets of water pelted my rain suit. Undeterred, I trudged among the graves, searching for the Baloun name. I only had this one opportunity.

Mire and slosh splattered my legs, and my shoes sank deep, slurping as I struggled to lift them. My weakened muscles made my quest more difficult.

Shielding my eyes from a thick watery veil of rain, I studied tombstone after tombstone. Many had plaques placed at the top, housing a memento symbolizing something especially revered by the deceased. A photo of children or a spouse. A pet. A star. A polished stone. I imagined the tears that must have splattered each token's tender placement, left by mourners who weren't ready to say goodbye.

Considering the people represented by each memorial, I thought of my own failing body — and the potential impact for my family. I swept tears off my cheek, disguised as drops of rain.

A groundskeeper came along, shouting over the thunder.

Our female driver who doubled as a translator, cupped her hands to amplify her voice and interpreted in English, "He asks if you need help."

"We are looking for the burials of our family. Baloun." I yelled over a thunderous boom.

The caretaker's sigh was carried away with the wind before he continued in his native tongue.

My interpreter translated. "He says that is a problem. He does not recognize the name."

We continued our search anyway, examining over 300 grave sites. Yet we never located the resting places of our ancestors — we discovered later we were in the wrong location.

Years before, approximately a mile from our hunt, a church had exploded after munitions hidden by German Nazis during World War II, detonated. In addition to the church building, the blast destroyed much of the cemetery next to it. We learned the Baloun graves were likely among the decimated graves.

Not everything on our trip was disappointing though.

From Germany, we took a Viking River Cruise on the Elbe, one of Central Europe's major rivers. Feeling the fresh water breezes lift my hair gave me the sense I was breathing the same air as my ancestors. For a few liberating moments, vitality coursed through my veins, making me feel energized. The leaves on the trees appeared greener. The smells of the earth became stronger, as the boat's hull sliced through the Elbe's murky water.

Experiencing the region of my maternal roots made me feel vibrant and connected to the universe. I enjoyed learning how the linen factories in and around Klatovy helped guide my own destiny by way of their influence on the Baloun clan. As the area prospered through the transport of goods down the Danube, Elbe, and other rivers in the region, many from surrounding communities migrated to look for a better life in the emerging economy. The Baloun's among them.

My mother's full name was Lucille Dora Baloun Perkins. She was the daughter of Joseph F. and Eula Evans Baloun. Her father was born in St. Louis, Missouri on October 29, 1880. He was the only child of Joseph Wolfgang and Alina Bettingheimer Baloun.

Joseph Wolfgang immigrated to the United States in 1872, before he turned eighteen — possibly sent by his parents to escape the tyranny of the ruling Hapsburg regime and the constricting demands of the European Catholic Church. Great-grandfather Baloun was born in Klatovy, Bohemia.

Joseph Wolfgang arrived in New York aboard the Donau, and ended up in St. Louis, where he became a U.S. citizen in 1877. Once Great-grandfather Baloun migrated to the United States, he invested family money and his European training as a skilled tailor and jeweler to set up shop in the Soulard section of St. Louis — made up of mostly middle-class eastern Europeans. It was there he became a successful businessman and property owner, until he lost most of his fortune in the stock market crash of 1929.

In addition to impeccable work ethics, my great-grandfather brought his religious beliefs with him when he crossed the ocean. He was an active member of the Free-Thinking Czech-Slavonic Benevolent Association, established in opposition to the religious constraints spurred by the injustices he'd left in Klatovy.

The Free-Thinking creed reveals that its followers believe in mankind, nature, and in the universe. Their religion has no church, denomination, building, or services structure. They believe in love, justice, science, and art, and played a foundational role in establishing the separation of the church and state in our national constitution.

Originally, the majority of freethinkers were agnostics, those who believe that nothing is known or can be known of the existence or nature of God or of anything beyond material phenomena; a person who claims neither faith nor disbelief in God. Their ideologies corresponded to those of Benjamin Franklin and Thomas Jefferson — freethinkers who generally put more faith in practical work than personal testimony.

Based on the free-thinking commitment to pragmatism, I wondered what my great-grandfather might have thought about what I witnessed when I died.

How would he respond to the impact my story is having on others for the kingdom of God? Would he have disregarded my testimony and called it emotional hogwash?

We might have debated over this one. I am not ashamed of how I feel after what I experienced. I know it was real, and I am emotional about it. By my "death," my life changed.

My trip to Prague and Klatovy caused me to appreciate my lineage in a deeper, more personal way. Sometimes I think we forget that what we enjoy today exists because of courageous pioneers from our past.

As a Free-Thinker and member of the Independent Order of Odd Fellows, when my great-grandfather, Joseph Wolfgang Baloun, came to America and started a family, he likely wanted proof of God's existence. Until I had my own *meeting with*

God moment, I too spent my life looking for evidence — yet the proof was all around me the whole time.

God authenticates His handiwork in the supernatural order of things. He designed the creatures who live in the great outdoors. His blueprint for life on our planet produced intricate and stunning flora. Time and elements were intricately scheduled. His fingerprints are obvious in the architect of mankind, all pointing to a masterful orchestration. Unfortunately for me, I would take much of this for granted, until my life was threatened. I ignored what I saw in every day detail.

When I was stripped of my health, I learned to see God's creation and discovered a greater appreciation for the invisible gifts that were passed on to me by others. The choices my ancestors made not only benefited them, but they paved the way for my own success.

The greatest inheritance I received wasn't money or possessions. Greater than gold, my family left me knowledge, skills, ambition, dedication, optimism, and a developing faith.

My visit to Klatovy educated me about my roots, but the trip was physically taxing. How I felt there was merely a hint of what I would soon face.

In 2009, I didn't yet know my heart disease was progressing, or how true Job's words would resound in my life. As it is recorded in the book of Job, "The Lord gives, and the Lord takes away" (Job 1:21 HCSB).

The Lord does give, and He does take away. But He also never abandons us in the healing process. Through my upcoming bouts with death, I was to learn that truth first-hand.

DEUTERONOMY 32:7 (NLT)
"Remember the days of long ago; think about the generations past. Ask your father, and he will inform you. Inquire of your elders, and they will tell you."

CHAPTER FIVE

Things Have Changed

Something was not right. When we returned home from Klatovy, I called my cardiologist's office and scheduled an appointment immediately. Dr. Dwyer ordered tests, adjusted my meds, and opened the door of discussion about another heart surgery in the future. For several months, he attempted to improve my condition, but nothing helped.

In March, 2011, my gall bladder was removed. But it didn't decrease my discomfort or address my other health problems.

My shortness of breath grew more intense, my energy waned, and my kidneys were beginning to fail. By July, I had a cardioversion, an electric shock to my heart, in hopes that it would improve my blood flow and reset my heart to a normal rhythm. But with a litany of issues, I continued to worsen.

My nephrologist, Dr. Juan Garcia, diagnosed chronic stage three kidney disease. My baseline creatinine was 1.8.

Creatinine is the waste product of muscular metabolism. Its normal range is 0.6-1.2 mg/dl, according to accepted standards, making my 1.8 level higher than healthy organs produce. In layman's terms, this indicated kidney damage of at least 50%, since my numbers were steadily increasing.

Added to my kidney problems were longstanding atrial fibrillation, hypertension, hypercholesterolemia, and trigeminal neuralgia. I didn't smoke, didn't abuse alcohol, and had no known allergies, yet my body was fighting itself. It was time to have another serious discussion with my doctor.

After many years under his care, Dr. Jerry Dwyer and I were more than doctor/patient. In the fall of 2011, he spoke to me with the professionalism of a physician, and the frankness of a friend.

"Your pacemaker has floated down, and you have severe mitral-regurgitation. Plus, your heart is still abnormally thick."

A cool wind blew outside, but as Dr. Dwyer spoke, the air inside seemed stodgy and dry. I felt like I was choking.

"Even though you had the bad valve replaced in 2002, we filleted some of the thickness off your heart muscle, and we installed the pacemaker, your hypertrophic cardiomyopathy is progressing. You've done functionally well, but I think it's time for heart surgery while you're body has the strength to handle it. Sixty-two is relatively young, but I have to tell you, you are a very sick dude."

His use of common-man language seemed to add credence to his professional assessment. Though I wasn't really scared, I did appreciate Dr. Dwyer's concerns. I returned home and reconsidered my plans for the future. If I had one.

I entered the hospital in November, 2011 for a cardiac catheterization the following day. The surgeon would also re-do my sternotomy, replace my mitral valve, and repair my tricuspid valve. Afterward, he would re-position my pacemaker to its proper setting.

It was as if I returned to my 2002 pre-surgical experience, although the procedure and the outcome post-surgery would prove dramatically different. I did not know what was about to happen.

After my family left for the evening, the night nurse fussed over me, checked my vitals and made sure all was in order. I tried to joke with her, "Hey, I think you missed a spot. You didn't poke me here." I pointed to a place on my arm, but she was all business. I did get a half-smile and a quick nod of agreement.

She eased the door shut behind her.

Left in solitude, there was nothing I could do, except reflect on God and my life. Sleep wasn't an option.

PSALM 143: 5 (NIV)
"I remember the days of long ago; I meditate on all your works and consider what your hands have done."

CHAPTER SIX

Harsh Climates and Deep Roots

We often avoid thoughts of death and dying until a crisis —
at least that was the case for me. But as I waited through the
hours before my surgery, all I could think about was my past,
and its impact on my after-life.

I pondered who I was, and I wondered how I'd ended up
in this hospital room. I was surrounded by beeping monitors,
stark white walls, and the pungent odor of strong disinfectant,
but my mind took me to other places.

Instead, I was whisked to a time where musty earth, manual labor, and a different way of defining success ruled. Where
harsh climates caused us to grow deep roots, but still allowed
us time to play. When I was young, living in the idealistic
country community of Steelville, Missouri.

When you want to know why you act the way you do, it's
good to look at your ancestors. A lot of their traits slip in, and
unless you slow down to think about it, you might not realize
the importance of the blood and genes that run through your
body.

Coming to the end of your life wakes you up to this fact.

I come from a long line of hard-scrapping folks. Ancestral names like Evans, Stilwell, Williams, Snoddy, Smith, and of course, Perkins.

My parents were products of the Great Depression, and they taught me to be thrifty. Dad's side of the family were primitive settlers in the Steelville area.

Tragedy and fortitude are foundational elements in the Perkins family. My Great-grandparents Perkins, William and Elizza, died prematurely in 1876 and 1877 respectively, orphaning their seven children, including John Washington Perkins, my granddad. Grandpa John was sent to live with a German family when he was around thirteen years old.

Family stories indicate that John ran away as a teenager, and found work on the new railroad. Other legends say he was robbed by the James and Younger Gang. No one knows for sure what happened to John between 1880 and 1896, before he surfaced in Steelville. For sixteen years, his life is pure mystery. We can only speculate.

Once Grandpa John settled in Steelville, he married my grandmother, Rebecca Snoddy, whose father Sam, fought for the Union during the American Civil War from 1861 to 1865. Grandpa John and Grandma Becky raised seven boys and one girl — my dad, Lawrence J. Perkins, nicknamed Tic, was one of their sons.

Grandpa and Grandma Perkins spent their lives farming in Crawford County, first on a small piece of rented land, and eventually on a place of their own, one hundred acres near Becky's childhood home. But life wasn't easy for them, especially when one of their young sons was killed while squirrel hunting for food.

Grandpa and grandma's bathroom was an outhouse, a wooden shack built around a hole in the center. Sears and Roebuck or J.C. Penney catalogues were used as toilet paper, pages torn as needed from the tissuey advertising sheets inside the thick books.

Out of necessity, most sicknesses were treated with home remedy, since doctors weren't near or affordable. Yes, life was tough on the Perkins' family, but instead of letting it pull them apart, they used adversity to draw them closer to each other.

When the children grew, they brought their families back to the farm on Sundays to visit. I played happily within that climate, learning to look for the positives, no matter what happened in life. One more thing that would help me get through my health crisis.

Mostly, Grandpa John would sit quietly on the porch. He was a watcher.

Grandma Becky was his polar opposite. Action followed her everywhere. She laughed and told her lively stories among the kitchen chaos of banging pans and pots.

Ann Donet, a nearby neighbor and author of *Two Hundred Years and Then Some*, said of my grandparents, "It is impossible to mention John or Becky alone. To do so would be unjust to the other. Aunt Becky did the talking, Uncle John did the listening, and she included him in every conversation by ending her statement with, "Isn't that right, John?"

I love the story Ann tells of someone asking Grandma Becky how she and Grandpa met. In Ann's book, she says, "A girlish smile crept across Aunt Becky's wrinkled face as her eyes focused on John. "Oh, in my earlier days I was good lookin' and had curves in all the right places. I had been to an outing and was getting ready to go home with my family when a nice-looking young man asked if he could walk me home. You know, it was dark out there and I really didn't have to think about it, but I did waste a little time acting like I was thinking about it before I said okay. Isn't that right John?"

Ann went on to say about Grandma, "Also, she never seemed to see the dull side of life. She would tell a sad story in such a way that she would have you smiling through your tears. If ever there was a couple who could boost the morale of younger people, the blue ribbon would have to go to Becky and John Perkins."

When I read this particular part about Grandma Becky, I think about myself. Many have described me in similar ways. I know from experience that you can smile and joke your way through big troubles. It helps you move through mean times, and my grandparents faced plenty.

Many of my mannerisms, habits, and attitudes came from my Grandma Becky. My love for story-telling and optimism are grounded in her legacy. But I've got some of Grandpa in me as well.

The things my Grandpa John gave me were a purposeful and pragmatic outlook, with a focus on leadership and healthy ambition. His influence was especially evident in my dad.

As a young husband and father, in addition to running our family's jewelry/sporting goods shop and working at the bank, my dad cut men's hair and hewed railroad ties to support his family. He seemed like a big man to me, at 6'1" who weighed about 240 pounds. He appeared to swing his ax with little effort.

For entertainment, he coon hunted and gigged fish at night, played basketball and baseball, or listened to boxing on the old radio that much of our family time centered around. While we sat at Dad's feet and followed the match, Mom and Grandma Baloun quilted, crocheted, darned socks to repair holes, or they played cards.

During the work week, Dad wore pressed and starched slacks with button up plaid shirts — his typical choice was blacks threaded with reds, blues, and yellows. He even wore them to the family farm, where he often went after a full work day in town.

In the summer, we had a big family garden. I think the

mental break provided by manual labor was therapeutic for Dad. He'd walk in the door, snatch his tan straw hat off its hook, and smoothly place it on his head for protection from the sun.

That old hat flopped in time with his swinging hoe as he weeded the rows around potatoes, carrots, onions, and corn. Because of his diligence in the garden, plus the cattle, chicken, and hogs we raised, we had plenty of food for the winter. Back then, a real man didn't rely on anyone else to take care of his family. He had to be reliable, responsible, and self-sufficient. He taught his children through hands-on experience provided through regular chores.

Dad was also a dedicated community member, attending most meetings held at his local Masonic lodge. Mom and Grandma were equally as committed to the Eastern Star group for women. While they were gone, we knew we'd better finish the tasks they left for us to do.

On special occasions, Dad dressed up, wearing a formal tie and suit. Extraordinary events such as a festive trip to watch the Cardinals play baseball in St. Louis, a trip by train or airplane, and every Sunday to church required special clothes. Sometimes he chose a swanky fedora hat. In his day, people wanted to appear respectable in public.

By the time I arrived, Dad had learned the craft of making and repairing fine jewelry from Grandpa Baloun, Mother's dad. Monday through Friday, 8 a.m. - 6 p.m., my father worked at our jewelry and sporting goods shop in town. He toiled over tiny watch mechanisms and squinted to set sparkling gems in gold bands.

In our family, you determined your own future by your choices to work and learn. Like many in our community, we were guided by the King James Version of the Bible in Proverbs 22:1, "A good name is rather to be chosen than great riches, and loving favor rather than silver and gold."

Steelville produced proud, practical people. When I was a kid, you labored until the job was complete — only then could you play and have fun.

But my favorite day of the week as a boy was Friday.

Our family faithfully celebrated the end of the week each Friday night. My father would load us into our 1953 Plymouth shortly after 6 p.m., and drive to Cuba, Missouri, about ten miles away.

I don't know what made us three boys bounce more — our excitement or the bumpy ride in our old car. No matter how difficult the week, we looked forward to our Friday night ride.

Once in Cuba, our dad often got us an ice cream to eat while we waited in the car so he could go inside Heiney's Bar. Sometimes he bought all of us boys a soda and a bag of chips or pretzels. After we got our goodies, he'd return to the bar for two cold glasses of beer, extending his stay on nights when the Gillette Cavalcade of Sports played boxing matches on the small set behind the counter.

He didn't go to bars much, and he never kept beer in the ice box at home, but every Friday we could count on Dad's routine — and our weekly entertainment.

Once Dad finished, he'd join us in time to watch the Frisco train rumble by for entertainment. Though we knew what to expect, each week we still anticipated the slow-building tremor that shook the ground. When the squeal of metal against metal sounded, before the rust-red train cars came into view, we'd lock eyes with the lone massive headlight peering ahead of the screeching locomotive. The train had finally arrived.

Some nights, we'd get a wave from the engineer, leaning out the open window. It was a slower time with my brothers and dad. I miss those days.

As I lay in my hospital bed reminiscing, I realized it was the predictable things that made my childhood special. Play. Family security. Chores. My parents didn't request my coop-eration — it was a requirement, and a necessity.

I remember Dad as a good listener, a natural encourager who motivated us with rewards, but who didn't shy away from discipline. He was confident and firm when he spoke.

Along with my two older brothers, Joe and John, I learned to drive at the farm, before any of us reached legal age. Because he lived through The Great Depression, Dad was prudent. Our father drilled into us the need to drive cautiously, making sure we avoided running over rocks. In Dad's youth, rubber tires were an expensive luxury.

Before we were allowed to accelerate down our dusty farm road, he'd admonish, "Son, those tires are hard to come by and awfully expensive. You be careful, 'cause we can't afford to replace 'em."

Even now, I still watch for rocks when I drive.

Though Dad didn't finish college himself, he pushed all his sons to get their degrees in higher education. He and my mother worked hard to make sure we were exposed to the vast world beyond Crawford County, Missouri.

Both of my parents were caring people. As a schoolteacher, Mom brought students home, and tutored them after feeding them a warm meal from our table. Not only did she pour arithmetic, reading, writing, and world studies into their minds, but she also taught them the value of doing a job well and seeing it to completion. As her children, we got to hear it twice — once for her students, and once spoken directly to us. As the youngest, born when Mom was forty-two, I think she added bonus material for me. I probably needed it.

Mom was frugal in her spending, and systematic in her routines. On Monday's, you could count on ham hocks and beans for supper, slow cooked all day in our Griswold cast iron pot. With the beans, she served steaming cornbread with locally made molasses drizzled over the top. Complaints were not allowed. We had to clear our plates.

Refusing food was not an option. Whether it was squirrel, polk greens, or homemade blackberry cobbler, you ate it, and you liked it.

Monday was also wash day — when we got fresh clothes to wear. Grandma Baloun lived next door, and she came to help Mom scrub our gritty blue jeans on wooden wash boards.

After a thorough hand scour, they'd crank the denim through our wringer washer. Even when cleaning, Mom and Grandma made sure they looked their best, dressed in blue cornflower or pink rose dusted dresses, purchased from Irv Noodleman's Mercantile.

You could tell they were related, as they both had a habit of smoothing strands of hair neatly into place, ensuring their weekly beauty parlor hairdo was maintained. "Never know who's likely to show up," they'd say.

Because my grandfather and dad were both jewelers, their wives never wore costume jewelry. Mom and Grandma often donned pearl necklaces with sapphire or opal clip-on earrings. My mother and grandmother were quite the duo — country dames — a mix of hard workers and refined ladies.

While doing the most strenuous of chores, silken slips sometimes snuck past the hemline of their blue or pink utility dresses. Mom and Grandma Baloun hung our clothes on long lines of thin, white rope, until sweat cascaded off their faces.

I thought about the effort my mom and her mom put into washing our heavy-duty bluejeans. Yanking and tugging, Mom and Grandma pushed wire stretchers inside the denim to make sure the legs were straight and neat while they dried. More than once they chided, "Can't have you looking a mess."

With their hands placed on their hips, they scolded, "Don't get dirty, there will be no clean clothes until Monday."

There's no telling what we swiped into our pants legs as we

layered a week's worth of grime into those fibers.

As much as Monday's were regimented, so were weekends. We got our weekly scrubbing in the bathtub Saturday night, so the dirt was washed away before we went to church on Sunday. Crisp and clean, our whole family attended worship service together. Dad wore his suit and shined-up shoes. Mom and Grandma put on their Sunday go-to-meeting dresses — they only wore hats on holidays like Easter.

Faith, family, and work were the foundation of our existence.

After church, we could count on pan-fried chicken, freshly-baked dinner rolls, green beans or corn, sliced red tomatoes and cucumbers in the summer, homemade mashed potatoes, and Mom's special chicken gravy for lunch. Fresh brewed iced tea washed down our meal. Because everything was made from scratch, our Sunday meal time was 2 p.m.

When they hollered, "Come and get it," we all came running.

My mouth still waters when I remember those country meals. What we get from today's grocery store shelves doesn't compare — there's nothing like a home-cooked meal where everything is made from food cultivated and prepared by your own hands.

In those days, nothing was wasted. We found a use for everything. When the ice man drove down the street with his massive, frozen blocks, we kids were there to get a treat. As he deftly measured and sliced squares to fit the the exact cut for every ice box on his route, we snatched up the fragments. They soothed our hot tongues on sweltering summer days.

In summers, we pricked our fingers picking blackberries and gooseberries. We raised cattle and butchered our own hogs and chickens. As much of a lady as my mom was, she was swift and determined when necessary. She could break the neck of a chicken with a single snap, in order to kill it mercifully. Life dictated sacrifice and understanding.

A knock on the door interrupted my memories, drawing my attention back to the hospital room. The nurse measured my blood pressure and temperature, then replaced the bag for my IV drip. Afterwards, she slipped out the door — and I returned to thoughts of my past.

As kids we saw an osteopathic doctor who lived across the street from us. But Mom and Grandma used an occasional home remedy like Castor Oil or Mercurochrome — the cures for all stomach pain and minor cuts. As I reminisced from my hospital bed, I wished Mom was there to treat my heart.

When I was a kid, Mom was as thrifty with her language as she was with medicine, money, and material resources. She always used proper English, and demanded we do the same. Though we lived in a rural community, my mother would never say, "ain't." She was a dedicated school teacher and a stickler for good grammar.

Mom also had strict requirements for us, even when what we wanted didn't line up with her plans. She wanted me to be a piano player, but my fingers were thick and I was far too impatient to sit and practice. I wanted to play on my dirt and gravel covered court, where a bare, metal-ring basketball hoop hung.

My childhood obsession was basketball. It birthed an athletic passion that prepared me for a bigger game — the game of my life.

Like all challenging sporting events, life doesn't always play out like we plan. Just when we think we have things figured out, the rules change, forcing us to rebound from losses and threatening defeats.

I glanced at the hospital clock on the wall, and it reminded me of a shot-clock counting down. I looked at the minute and hour hands on the black sphere. In less than six hours the medical team would come for me. I wasn't afraid, but I couldn't turn off my reflective thinking. My body was tired, but I would sleep during surgery. My brain was wide awake, considering a myriad of outcomes.

2 TIMOTHY 1:7 (NLT)
"For God has not given us a spirit of fear and timidity, but of power, love, and self-discipline."

CHAPTER SEVEN

Snippets of Earth and Heaven

Life doesn't provide much time for self-examination. Prior to my illness, the busyness of my own routines prevented me from thinking about my childhood much. But as I waited for the hours to pass until my surgical team prepped me, I allowed myself to tip-toe back through the days of my youth.

I was born in 1948, when my mom was in her early forties. An unusual situation for the era. Like my older brothers, I lived with Grandma Baloun for several years. We took care of her after my grandfather died.

As a young man, Grandpa Baloun attended a trade school in St. Louis and learned the trade of watch-making. After moving to Steelville, he met Eula Augusta Evans, my maternal grandmother, who was born October 31, 1888. She was the daughter of the circuit court clerk and recorder of deeds, William C. Evans — a Civil War veteran who fought for the Union. A man who obviously had a softer side as well.

In a letter dated, December 23, 1907, with deep emotion, my Great-grandfather Evans sent the following note to his soon-to-be-married girl — days before her wedding.

> *Steelville, MO*
> *Miss Eula Evans*
>
> *Dear Daughter:*
> *This may be the last letter that I will ever address to*
> *"Miss Eula Evans." The thought is sad; yet I hope that the*
> *name you will soon assume may lead you to a life of hap-*
> *piness founded on a Love that can never be broken. This*
> *is the earnest wish of*
> > *Your affectionate "Papa",*
> > *Wm. C. Evans*

My grandpa, Joseph F. Baloun, married my grandmother, Eula Evans, on January 1, 1908, at her family home.

Mom and Dad purchased the lot next door to Grandpa and Grandma Baloun near the intersection of Oak Street and Shady Lane in Steelville. My parents eventually built a stone house on the lot — the house I grew up in. As close as we were with our grandparents, I guess you could say we almost lived communally.

Our stone house saw generations come and generations depart. As a boy, I lived there when stars still twinkled under darkened skies, without light pollution dulling their glow. Though our house was in town, crickets chirped, peep frogs sang, and whippoorwills twilled, free to harmonize without the rude interruptions of civilized life. You might say we were the Mayberry of Missouri — all we needed was Andy Griffith.

Steelville rarely saw serious crimes. Compared to other parts of the world, including neighborhoods within a few miles, our community is still considered relatively safe.

When I was a kid, on Saturday nights, we'd go to the one room movie theater on Main Street. For a dime, we could watch world reports, followed by a Tom and Jerry cartoon, before watching the big attraction. Ma & Pa Kettle movies were favorites, even though they were shown in black and white.

I liked the part where Ma Kettle stood on their dilapidated porch and hollered at her big brood, "Come and get it."

A rush of feet, sounding like hooves, trampled from all corners of their sad-looking farm. A door would splinter off its hinges, or a cabinet might fall off the wall, but whatever broke, Pa would keep rocking in his chair, unruffled.

In his even-tempered tone, he'd say, "Ma, I'm gonna have to fix that one of these days." Then he'd puff smoke from his pipe and rock some more.

No matter what they faced, by the end of the movie, the Kettle clan found something to laugh about, and they banded together. In some ways, they reminded me of my family. But my dad never slacked, our home was always tidy, and we didn't have a dozen kids. But many of the scenes on the screen did mirror our general sense of simple tranquility.

My parents didn't worry about sending us to the movies alone — even when I was only five or six. Only two things concerned me — the long walk to the theater, and having to visit the restroom. Scary things lurked in those places.

Bullies have always existed — even in the peaceful time of my childhood. It didn't take many frights in the shadows of night to learn what to avoid.

Older boys hid behind the immense oak trees lining the side street that connect with Main. Evening after evening, they waited to startle younger kids walking by. Snickering and whispering plots amongst themselves, they'd wait until the precise moment of greatest impact, then, "BOO!" — they'd jump out and scare the snot out of us.

Once I arrived at the theater, I relaxed, at least until I needed to use the bathroom. I learned quickly not to go where the mean boys hung out. They were the same ones who hid behind the trees. Thick smoke swirled and cloistered the air, exhaled from cigarettes they stole from their dads and uncles. Those of us who were younger feared what they might do to us in the bathroom.

Fortunately for me, Irv Noodleman's Mercantile, next to the theater, was always open when I needed it. His general store — the same shop where Mom and Grandma Baloun bought their blue cornflower and pink rose sprinkled dresses — was a refuge from the bullies for me.

Irv was always there long after dark. I assume he expected customers would need one of his wares. But Irv was a kind soul, and he often let me sneak over to use the tiny restroom located in the back corner of his store. The big boys never thought to look for me there.

I learned from Irv that kindness and compassion from a business owner can turn customers into friends. Irv also sold great toys and bicycles — though our playthings didn't usually come from his store.

We used imagination and effort to create our fun. Cowboys attacked Indians with hand-carved pistols made from sticks of wood. We built tree houses in back yards, and forts out of abandoned fence posts. Adventure was a daily possibility. Comic heroes like Superman and Buck Rogers took us to galaxies beyond time and space. We bounced balls on clay courts. Our un-netted basketball hoops were bent circles of steel. At the time, we didn't realize how much pretending was training us for real life.

On hot days, we visited the local drugstore with chrome barstools covered in red vinyl. Palm leaf ceiling fans rotated above our heads. We cooled down with ice cream sodas, hand-dipped by the soda jerk behind the counter.

Coke signs and Rosie the Riveter posters adorned the walls. The owner was a pharmacist named Slick Lichius, and his personality was as comical as his name. He entertained us with boisterous stories and bawdy jokes. He grinned and nodded his head as he took the nickels we shoved across the green speckled countertop in exchange for frosty glasses of cherry soda.

In the background from the juke box, Patti Page sometimes asked, "How Much is that Doggie in the Window?" Crooner Perry Como, belted out, "Don't Let the Stars Get in Your Eyes." Doris Day sang, "Anna." And Tony Bennett's emphatic songbird promise in "Rags to Riches" gave us hope for a brighter tomorrow.

Some of that music was pointing me to a future, far, far away. Secrets to reveal — snippets of Earth and Heaven.

This wonderful phase of my life passed too quickly, like an evaporating mist. But not before I met my forever love, the girl who captured my heart and still holds me captive. This woman saved me from myself many times over.

JAMES 4:14 (NIV)
"Why, you do not even know what will happen tomorrow.
What is your life? You are a mist that appears for a little while
and then vanishes."

CHAPTER EIGHT

Forever Sweethearts

As I waited in my hospital bed, ignoring my current condition while remembering my past, a girl's face floated into my mind.

How could I review my blessings without focusing on my wife, Linda? Of all the gifts God has given me, she is the best. I know a lot of men say they don't deserve the woman they married. But when life-threatening disease occurs, not all women stand by their men. Thankfully, my wife was always by my side.

I met my wife in high school, when all I thought about were my studies and basketball. But the right girl turned my head, melted my heart, and changed my way of thinking.

My cousin, Bob, was a close friend. I leaned over one day during band practice and asked him, "Who's that girl in the clarinet section?"

"Some new girl," he grinned at me.

In a daydream state I drawled, "She's purty."

After that day, I made it my mission to get to know her.

At first, Linda ignored me. She was shy and I was not exactly handsome. We weren't the typical couple who would launch a lifelong romance. But Mother Nature helped me out with a substantial snowfall.

My cousin Bob and I, along with our friend, Connie Wright, decided to ride snow sleds. Connie brought her cousin along — and I'm sure you can guess her name — Linda. The purty girl from the clarinet section.

My eyes lit up when I saw her. Even though the weather was frigid, I felt toasty inside. I made her my conquest — before the day was over, I hoped to win her heart.

In Steelville, we were all familiar with Rhea's Hill. Its curved slope was perfect for a fast, downhill sled ride. The long, bumpy surface made it even better when the right girl was seated behind you, gripping your waist. I arranged to have Linda sit behind me.

Half-frozen, we laughed the whole time. Over and over we challenged Rhea's Hill. By the end of the day, I knew Linda was the one. I had to make her mine. She wasn't yet convinced, but I was determined.

After our sledding day ended, I repeatedly asked her out. But while she was shy, Linda was no pushover. The more she turned me down — the deeper her hook was embedded in my heart.

It took weeks for her to agree, but finally, she said, "Yes."

I took her bowling on our first date. We had fun, in spite of my competitive nature. I wasn't going to let anyone beat me — I'm not that kind of guy — no matter how much I liked her, I needed to be the best.

Later, we dated exclusively, spending much of our time together playing double-deck Pinochle with Linda's dad and stepmom. Boys against the girls. Her dad and I usually beat them, but I'm sure I didn't handle the wins with grace.

I think our card games caused Linda to question her wisdom in dating me a few times. She quickly learned how much I needed to win.

In my youth, I didn't understand the art of putting someone I cared about ahead of my desire to succeed. I could have saved us both more anguish by withholding my obnoxious comments. It's bad enough when someone beats you, but when they constantly remind you, it is like rubbing salt in an open sore. Back then, I didn't realize that. I was young and brash, and my offensive sense of humor was not well-received or appreciated.

Through our years together, we have both grown wiser. I work hard to restrain myself now, but occasionally the old patterns rise to the surface. However, when it does, Linda is no longer afraid to call me out, she puts me back in a more respectful place. She had to do that many times during my lengthy illness.

Thankfully, she stayed with this cocky kid. We became high school sweethearts, and she still tugs my heartstrings today.

When we married in 1969, Linda had my ring engraved inside the band. The inscription reads, "LCF to PEP love forever. 1969." It stands for, "Linda Carol Frazee to Paul Edward Perkins. Love forever."

Ring etching is an intriguing thing. The durability of an engraving done on the outside of a ring depends on the durability of the metal itself. On softer metals, like gold, the ring will scratch and the engraving will wear away over time. But on hard metals like tungsten, the engraving will not wear down easily, and it's difficult to scratch.

Engravings on the inside of a ring will not fade, no matter what metal you choose. For the engraving to wear away, it would mean the skin was tougher than the metal.

The softness a ring is placed against is what protects the inscription, just as my wife's softness has protected our relationship. It isn't the wear people see on the outside of our marriage, but the softness of my wife against the hard surface of adversity, that maintains the heartbeat of our love.

My wedding ring remains as a strong reminder of our lives together. Linda is the strength behind my success and survival. We've lived in both a tiny mobile home and a large, spacious house. We've wondered what we could scrounge up to eat, and we've feasted on decadent meals. We've endured through sickness and health. We've faced death many times. Through it all, like Christ, no matter how obnoxious I was, my wife stayed faithful to me.

Our love is like the softness of skin protecting the symbol of our commitment from the harshness of life. Tested and tried, we are sure it will last forever.

Linda wasn't originally from Steelville. Her family chose this town over several others.

Tragedy struck when my wife was only five years old.

The night was dark. The rain heavy. A drunk driver sped over a hill and struck their car — with the entire family inside.

Their car careened off the highway into a deep ditch. Two were killed. Linda's mother and younger sister lost their lives.

I'm sure the inner strength Linda manifests today comes from surviving sorrowful experiences. She is a woman who knows what it's like to face trauma head-on. And how to bury her fears while caring for others during hard times. I never met her mother, but I imagine Linda inherited her tenacity.

Linda's father eventually remarried. Betty developed a deep love for Linda, but Linda's dad, Warren, impacted her most. She was blessed with a nurturing father. I aspire to give my children his level of wisdom and care.

Warren was a great man with high moral values. We never exchanged a cross word. He shared with me how difficult it was to forgive the man who took his wife and child. But through a determined decision-making process that required time and effort, he eventually released the bitterness and anger he harbored. Warren forgave him.

More than once, when someone hurt me, I remembered Warren, realizing if he could forgive someone for killing his wife and daughter, I could do the same for a slight or unkind word. What I learned from Warren about avoiding self-pity, instead of clutching it tighter, later served me when my life was in jeopardy.

It also made me aware of how many times his daughter had pardoned my failings as a husband. She always found a way to forgive me.

Her commitment and finesse in being my soft place to land during hard times was crucial for me. God knew I'd need a wife like Linda. Things were going to get rougher. It wasn't my first experience believing Someone was orchestrating my life.

PROVERBS 18:22 (NKJV)
*"He who finds a wife finds a good thing,
and obtains favor from the Lord."*

CHAPTER NINE

I'm Not Coming Back

I was fresh out of high school during the Vietnam era. The air we breathed smelled of conflict, chaos, and confusion in America.

Courage was required — for those who were sent to war and for those remaining on American soil. I planned to meet my draft obligation with the dignity and integrity demonstrated by my older brothers, Joe and John, as a proud officer of the United States Army. My brothers told me an officer's life expectancy in a Vietnamese fire fight was thirty-eight seconds. I rushed to marry Linda before becoming a soldier, aware of the challenges ahead.

I knew why I fell for her, but I couldn't comprehend why this shy and beautiful young woman fell for me. I was simply grateful she did.

My brothers served two years in Vietnam simultaneously, so the Army wouldn't deploy me immediately. I thought this would provide a year with my wife before I was sent to fight. I didn't tell her, but I was strategizing, knowing I might not return from battle.

In preparation for my stint in the Vietnam conflict, knowing the odds were not in my favor, I wanted to make sure my bride wasn't left destitute. So I encouraged her to find a good job, and I supported her efforts.

I am a strong extrovert. Linda is a deep introvert. As different as high waves and calm seas, we ebb and flow, balancing each other. This became evident early in our marriage.

Following our wedding, Linda applied for a teaching position. During the interview process, they explained that the pay was $5,800 a year. The median family income in 1971 was $10,600. The annual U.S. inflation rate was 4.3%. An average house cost $25,250, a gallon of gas — $0.40, and a jar of Jiffy peanut butter — $0.59. You could get your little girl a Malibu Barbie for only $1.94.

According to the National Center for Education Statistics, the average pay for an elementary teacher in 1971 was $9,021. I knew my brilliant wife deserved better than $5,800. So when Linda told me about the offer, I said to her, "Stay here, I'll be right back."

I vaulted up the steps and asked to speak with the woman in charge of the selection process. I introduced myself. "Hi, I'm Paul Perkins, and I want to thank you for interviewing my wife. I understand there are several applicants."

She smiled and said, "Yes there are. But you'll have to wait until the specified date and time to find out the results."

She misunderstood why I'd asked.

I looked her in the eye and said, "I'd sure appreciate it if you'd take my wife's name off of your application list."

Her eyes widened, her mouth opened, and I heard her draw a deep breath, as I turned and left her speechless.

When I told Linda about my decision on her behalf, she said, "Why did you do that?"

I bristled, "You can find a better job for $5,800 a year."

I'm not sure she agreed. At that time, I believed in Linda's abilities more than she did.

Today, the same scenario would have produced very different results. My wife is much more sure of herself, and I've learned I'm better off when I listen to what she has to say.

Soon after, Linda was hired by the K-Mart corporation. She'd finished college in three years with a degree in Mathematics Education. It didn't take her employers long to discover they'd hired someone with great potential. So my wife moved up the corporate ladder quickly.

While she supported us, I worked on my M.B.A. in finance at the University of Missouri in Columbia, also known as Mizzou. It took me a full year and another summer to complete my thirty-six hour program for the degree.

On the heels of celebration, Linda and I were driven back to reality by a piercing update from the Army.

A letter came in the mail saying my brother John was coming home and my orders for Vietnam were in process. My time with my wife had expired.

While I waited for fate to ship me across the sea, it first directed me to Fort Benjamin Harrison, Indiana, to a division of the U.S. Army, called the Finance Corps. Since I'd received my B.S. in finance with a M.B.A., it was a natural fit. At a time when the Army only placed approximately 1,800 men in financial officer positions, it was a great honor.

My role was to do the complex work of converting a soldier's base salary, additional stipends, housing per diem, and other income allotments, into a Leave and Earnings Statement. All military personnel would receive this document, reflecting income, and showing their payroll deductions. Some items were taxable, and some were exempt, but military accuracy was required in all. I did not understand that these days were preparing me for my future. But first, I had to face my impending assignment to Vietnam.

Once again, I received notification to prepare myself. The time had come. More than once the thought crossed my mind, *I'm not coming back.*

But I was wrong.

Just before it was time for me to deploy, President Richard M. Nixon brought all of the troops home. It seemed as if my life was following a grand script, but I wasn't the one writing it.

My plans were to follow the paths of my brothers, Joe, who retired after twenty years as a Lieutenant Colonel and John, a Green Beret Captain, who would later serve at high levels in the CIA. The Army had commissioned me as a Second Lieutenant. And if I survived Vietnam, I was prepared for a career in the Army. But something guided me away from that war, likely sparing my life and changing the course of my future.

Due to events beyond my control, my time on Earth was extended. But I would still face Heaven early — except instead of leaving my body on a battlefield, I'd leave it in a hospital. And I would experience death more than once.

In the early hours of a cool November, 2011 morning, as I was wheeled down the corridor, I felt confident and ready for surgery. I had reviewed my life, made peace with God, and trusted Him to pull me through quickly.

Instead, death caught up with me under a surgeon's knife in St. Louis. I hadn't seen it coming.

ROMANS 8:28 (ESV)
"And we know that for those who love
God all things work together for good, for those
who are called according to his purpose."

CHAPTER TEN

My First Death

Worry did not accompany me into the operating room that November. Not that it was a routine procedure, but I was confident in the medical team and their abilities. In a top St. Louis hospital, they were head of the class. They made sure I understood the risks, and I appreciated their commitment to honesty, but as I was wheeled into the operating room, I chose to ignore the warnings and focused on a positive potential outcome.

Under a wall of anesthesia, I felt no pain. Even when the unplanned occurred.

My wife, Linda, children, Mark, Julie, and Scott, as well as my sisters-in-law, Donna, Lisa, and Laurie, and my niece Tracie, passed the time in the surgery suite waiting room. My daughter Julie's best friend, Anne Buchanan, also sat with us.

During times of intense stress, Anne's faith and encouragement provided a beacon of hope for Julie and our whole family. In 2011, on the Wednesday before Thanksgiving, Anne dropped everything and drove from Springfield, Missouri to

St. Louis, over three hours, to become our number one prayer warrior. She was a rock, the human force my family relied on to carry them to the strength of Jesus when I was at my weakest.

Linda tracked the details of my progress by carefully documenting updates journal-style as they were given.

Her first entry read:

Hospital Log: Day 1 — Tuesday, November 22, 2011

The doctor called after 11:00 and said, "It's going slow while we get through the scar tissue. We had to snip tissue from the shaft and other areas."

Several long hours passed before they heard anything else. When they did, Linda dutifully wrote it down.

We finally heard from the doctor at 3:00. He said it would be another hour. He called again at 4:30 and said you were bleeding. So far, they weren't able to locate the source. You didn't get out of surgery until eightish. By 10:00, they had to take you back to the operating room to repack and check for blood clotting. You were in surgery over twelve hours.

Before they could begin your heart work, the doctors first had to remove lots of scar tissue. This took nearly an hour, delaying the beginning of your procedure.

During the echocardiogram, they saw bleeding and had to determine where the bleed was coming from, it took them thirty minutes to find it. According to the surgeons, blood was oozing everywhere, and was very difficult to clot. It turned out your pulmonary artery was clipped, but at first, they couldn't determine exactly where. This was a very dangerous situation, they had to find where your artery was cut. Once they finally located the bleed, it had to be repaired quickly, before it was too late. They grafted it once and patched the artery and graft. But it didn't

take. All three surgeons were working to try and save you.
They grafted and packed again, it finally took this time.
They also had to repair your tricuspid and replace your
mitral-valve.

You were given a lot of blood today, and were on the
heart/lung machine for seven hours.

Your chest is still open, and your first night in the
Cardio Vascular Unit was difficult. All night, five nurses,
and Dr. Mauney watched you closely.

You are swollen with lots of fluids.

My family didn't find out until later just how bad things
were in the operating room. During the delicate procedure,
one of my arteries was accidentally nicked, severing its protective skin and causing a massive bleed. From what the medical
team told us afterward, it took extensive effort to find and repair the source.

Later, Dr. Mauney told me, "There is no scientific reason to
explain how you are still here, or how your mental capabilities
are still intact." He shook his head in wonder, "It's really quite
incredible."

Dr. Dwyer reported that I clinically died in the operating
room.

When he was later questioned about the validity of my
death, Dr. Dwyer's answer was swift and sure. "Paul Perkins
died at least two medically confirmed times."

When it happened, I knew nothing of the life-threatening
complication, because while the doctors and nurses fought to
revive me, I was transported to another world. A world free
of pain or sorrow. I felt as if I were floating in the air, without
the heaviness of my body to hold me down. There were no
lights. I saw no tunnel. There was no essence of time passing.
Suddenly, my spirit left my body, and I was instantly somewhere else. It was both liberating and exhilarating.

In a place I can only assume to be Heaven, I felt God's presence, although I didn't see Him. I suppose I wasn't meant to stay yet. But I did see familiar people.

Though I hadn't seen them in many years, I recognized every person before me. It's hard to explain how they looked entirely different, yet exactly the same. None wore sad faces. Inside and out, they exuded pure joy.

The first person I approached was Grandma Baloun. But it was more than seeing her — it was as if we shared spirits and experiences together. We were immediately back at her house, like we were re-inhabiting the period I lived with her after Grandpa died.

We entered the screened-in sleeping porch, above the attic in her house. As a boy I spent many nights in that room.

I slept in a twin bed made of brass colored metal, with round knobs at the top of each of the four corners. Vertical slats were welded next to each other into the flat see-through headboard. I kept my baseball and football cards tucked beneath my thin mattress. The special ones were thumbtacked to the wall behind my bed.

Grandma had an identical twin bed on the opposite side of the room. Many nights over the crescendo of crickets, and under the illumination of the moon and stars, we would reminisce about the day's events. Sometimes swapping stories, sometimes letting silence speak on our behalf.

I melted into the comfort of familiar surroundings with Grandma. There is nothing on earth I can compare it to. Though I was still floating in this other-worldly paradise — I was at the same time back in the security of my childhood home. Yet, the surprises weren't over.

In less time than it takes to blink an eye, we joined my parents at their house. It was so good to see my mom. She greeted me with a huge smile. Dad looked young, vibrant, and happy.

I don't recall specific conversation, but we communicated with each other in a language of love. Our hearts did the speaking, instead of our voices.

While in this paradise, I had a wonderful time with my relatives. It was like the grandest celebration I've ever attended. It was euphoria at a level I'd never known — a sense of well-being that infiltrated every fiber of my spirit. It felt so good, I didn't want it to stop. I had no desire to re-enter my body. I yearned to stay in that place forever.

I feel guilty for saying this now that I'm back here on earth. But when I was there, I simply didn't want to return. I'm happy that I'm reunited with my wife and children, but there's a part of me that still longs for what I know is my true destination.

Through my experience, I know with certainty what those who accept Jesus Christ as their Savior and choose Heaven as their eternal home can expect upon death. I did not want to leave that supernatural atmosphere.

I don't remember the process of returning to my body. It was as if one moment I was enjoying the thrill of eternity, and the next I was back in the hospital.

Later, after I woke up from many days of unconsciousness, I realized an incredible fact about my Heaven experience. While I was in the spiritual realm, I did not worry about my wife, children, or grandchildren. They are typically foremost in my thinking, so this was unusual for me. But because of the sense of peace and security I felt while there, I didn't realize they *weren't* on my mind.

I can tell you with complete assurance, the best comes after we die — and I have no fear in crossing the threshold of death again. Frankly, I can't wait, even though I'm equally satisfied to complete my purpose on earth. Waiting on God's perfect timing means I won't miss out on anything He's planned for me.

Out of it in my hospital bed the first night, I didn't know what I would have to climb through in order to scale the pinnacle of healing. It would take longer than the doctors predicted, and several events would plunge me into a depth of despair I didn't know existed.

I didn't tell anyone what I experienced when I saw my family in Heaven. I wasn't sure what they would think. And besides, I didn't have time. Unbeknownst to me, a creeping blackness quickly approached — things were going to become ugly — and very intense.

JOB 13:15A (NKJV)
"Though He slay me, yet will I trust Him."

CHAPTER ELEVEN

61 Days of Hell

The second day of my hospital stay was the day before Thanksgiving — I spent my holiday in ICU. The doctors had left my chest flayed open, packed with sterile, bulky dressing to stave off bleeding and help with my blood pressure. I was aware of nothing.

A sheet was draped over me, so no one but medical personnel could see the white gauze inside my open chest. But it still must have been a shock for my family.

I was in critical condition, unable to breathe on my own, so a ventilator pumped air in and out of my lungs. None of us knew I would languish for sixty-one days in the hospital, making it a holiday season my wife and kids would never forget, and one I would never remember.

As my family prepared to settle into the Intensive Care waiting room at the end of my second day, they realized too late no one had brought overnight supplies. My niece, Tracie, volunteered to run to the nearest discount store where she bought underwear, t-shirts, toothbrushes, paste, gum, and other essentials to hold them over.

After she returned, everyone freshened up, settled in, and took various positions of rest around the waiting room. I'm not sure any of us had slept long, when just after 2:00 a.m., Dr. Mauney entered and shook my son, Mark, who was sleeping on a couch. Mark was groggy, and in his exhausted state, fought the intrusion.

Dr. Mauney shook him again and said, "You need to wake up. Your father's dying."

Mark jolted upright. After stirring Linda, the two of them woke everyone else in the room. It took several seconds for them to roust my other two kids and Julie's friend Anne.

Wearing a grim expression beneath furrowed eyebrows, Dr. Mauney took only enough time to summarize. "I'll know more once we get him into surgery, but his situation is dire. As soon as I have something to report, I'll be back to speak with you." He turned and strode through the doorway in clipped, efficient steps.

Mark thought, *I have to call Jerry Beers.*

Sleep was evident in Jerry's voice when he answered, but his conditioning as a pastor quickly shook the stupor from his words. When Mark explained what was happening, the family huddled around Mark's cell phone, and Jerry sprung into prayer.

Heavenly Father,

We thank you that nothing catches you off-guard. You said where two or more are gathered in your name, you would be in their midst, so Father, in Jesus' name, we lift Paul Perkins to you. You know the source of his medical problems, and we ask you to guide the hands and minds of the surgical team as you direct them to what needs to be fixed.

We ask you to comfort Paul's family. Blanket them with peace that passes all human understanding. Strengthen their faith, and help them lean into your grace. We praise you in ad-

vance for your perfect will. We entrust Paul into your wise and loving hands.

In Jesus' Mighty Name,

Amen

When my family looked up at the conclusion of the prayer, they saw a gurney blaze by with me on it. In the wee hours of Thanksgiving morning, my family clung to each other. Anne Buchanan and my niece Tracie, acted as prayer warriors, leading my family's ongoing petitions through the long wait.

Just before dawn, Dr. Mauney came into the family waiting area and said, "He's okay for now, but he's *very* sick. Actually, Mr. Perkins is a very sick man, the next few hours are critical. But even a slight chance for a good outcome is something for you to hold onto."

After he left, my family clung to the thin thread of optimism offered at the end of the doctor's statement.

Mark didn't cry, but he later admitted he felt nauseous. He said he kept hoping it was a bad dream they would wake up from. I'm sure the others felt much of the same.

My family didn't feel much like giving thanks on that dark holiday. Gloom draped their moods, and only worsened when my children had to make alternate arrangements for their own kids and spouses' Thanksgiving meals.

Scott and his wife Dawn, were supposed to host her entire family in their home that day. When Dawn rushed to the hospital to be by Scott's side, her family graciously watched Julie's children at Scott and Dawn's house, so Alex, Julie's husband, could come as well. Mark asked friends to take his boys in for the day, and they welcomed them without hesitation.

In the afternoon, once they put me on 100% oxygen, and I was placed on temporary dialysis, I stabilized, so my family went to the hospital cafeteria. Instead of sitting around a food-laden table with a crisp-crusted, juicy turkey, homemade dressing, and mounded dishes of delectable sides, my wife and children ate a bland Thanksgiving meal they said tasted like Band-aids. It was a definite low point.

The following day, my condition improved slightly. Around 7:00 p.m. that evening, a whole passel of visitors showed up. I wasn't awake, but the story they told me later was quite humorous.

One of our long-term bank employees, Wanda Grayson, noticed my foot was sticking out from beneath my blanket. She kindly moved the sheet to cover it.

Suddenly, the nurse snapped, "Don't touch him."

Wanda jumped back, thinking she'd done something really bad.

According to all reports, my entire room lit up with laughter, the nurse the loudest of all. But her humor didn't end there.

This part is kind of gross, but with a funny twist. Later that day, while still in my unconscious state, I finally relieved myself — making the doctor very happy.

He told my family, "The kind of bowel movement he had is unheard of. I'm very pleased."

My nurse looked at everyone in the room, then in all seriousness said, "It's what we call a Code Brown," then she broke out in laughter again. After her meaning connected in their brains, my family joined her. I guess it just proves they appreciate my ability to make them laugh — even when I'm not aware I'm doing it.

On my fifth day in the hospital, Dr. Mauney visited with my family early. He said, "He's improved a great deal over the past twelve hours. We've been able to remove over six pounds of fluid off of him in twenty-four hours. Our goal is to continue removing fluid over the next two days, while further weening him off of his blood pressure medications. We'll start him on a feeding tube shortly."

At 10:00 a.m., my blood pressure had dropped. The Mizzou/Kansas game was on the television in my room. Concerned it might agitate me, my family kept the volume down. My ever-creative and comedic nurse had a better idea.

"Turn the sound up. We need his blood pressure to rise, and maybe this will help."

Shortly after they increased the volume, Mizzou won the game, and my blood pressure shot into the desired range.

As my wife said, "Winning is good for my health."

My family rode a roller coaster of peaks and valleys for a while. Like the day the nursing staff said I'd had a good night and the doctor told them both the left and right sides of my heart were working well, only to have things drop to the bottom that same afternoon.

Dr. Mauney spoke to my family. "We were able to take both vents off. I didn't close his chest yet, the right side of his heart still appears to be struggling. His lungs are looking better though, so overall, I'm fairly pleased with the results. But the next twelve to twenty-four hours remain crucial."

By late afternoon, Linda and Julie were feeling uneasy about my condition. At 8:00 p.m., they were getting indications that there was more trouble regulating my blood pressure. At 10:30 that night, Dr. Mauney went to see them, but this time, he didn't have a great report.

"Paul has an infection. His temperature is currently 101 degrees, and he's in danger if his body can't fight it. I must be honest, there is a risk he could die from this."

When my wife and daughter saw me, they said a film of sweat covered my face.

Dr. Mauney increased the blood pressure medicine he referred to as my rocket fuel, and started me on three different antibiotics. Right before he left my room, he told Linda and Julie, "We'll know soon if the antibiotics will work."

My family described the mood as somber and smothering when Dr. Mauney walked out the door. It was clear things had taken another serious turn.

By morning, my body had responded well to the antibiotics, and Dr. Mauney was more optimistic. He gave my family a stern reminder. "He's doing better, but this is a marathon, and we still have a ways to go in this race."

Dr. Mauney further commented on my condition. "A week is the outside time limit for leaving a person's chest open, so I want to close him up this evening."

A short time later, Dr. Dwyer stopped by. He reviewed my infected tissue samples, and said my heart was working well. He told Linda, "I want to make sure his heart hardware continues to function optimally. I'll check in again once they've closed his chest." A tinge of worry laced his words when he added, "I'm concerned about the black spots on Paul's lips, fingers, and arms."

As hard as the situation was, knowing Dr. Dwyer was my friend as well as physician, gave my family comfort. So did my signs of improvement, especially when they removed the balloon pump. But things worsened shortly after 6:00 p.m.

Everyone except Linda, Mark, and my sister-in-law Lisa, had gone to eat dinner. The doctor came in, and in a tired voice reported, "Paul spiraled down again. Probably due to our trying to put in a line."

However, things peaked as quickly as they'd plummeted. I bounced back by 8:00. The medical staff said my numbers were the best yet. Linda later teased, "Knowing the prankster you are, I thought you were messing with my mind."

When the doctor came in for his final round, his demeanor was more energetic. He told Linda, "I think it's best if you all go to a hotel and get a good night's sleep. We're going to wait until tomorrow to close him up, and you'll do yourselves, each other, and Paul more good if you are rested. I have to admit, this case is like no other roller coaster I've ridden before."

Linda agreed.

On Wednesday, November 30, 2011, at approximately 7:45

a.m., Dr. Mauney sutured my chest shut after eight days of it being flayed open. He said he'd never had another patient open for that long. When he finished, he told my family, "Everything looked good and healthy with his heart and chest cavity. We've also isolated the bacteria that's been causing his infection. It's in his lungs and causing pneumonia.

Now that his chest is closed, his immune system should kick into high gear. Coupled with the appropriate antibiotics he's getting now, he at least has a fighting chance.

We've treated kidney failure all week, but now I think we're ready to adjust his treatment in a positive direction. I'm finally optimistic about his recovery. I think we're ready to try and bring him out of anesthesia."

Though I was still in my drug-induced coma, my family played football, Christmas carols, and Fox News on my ICU television. These were things I typically enjoyed, so they hoped something might touch a deep place in my soul, where they couldn't quite reach yet.

A skin specialist came in and looked at the black spots Dr. Dwyer was concerned about. She said she'd never seen anything like it, but thought my rocket fuel meds had pulled all the blood from my extremities and pooled it to my organs, causing the darkened areas to suffer from lack of blood flow or oxygen. It wasn't anything to be alarmed over.

My doctors slowly began reducing the sedatives keeping me under, and started me on a feeding tube again. I had a slight amount of jaundice, but the hospital staff said it was expected.

Dr. Mauney shared his enthusiasm on day ten — it was December 1st. "Overall, I'm pleased right now. You can't see all of the results on the outside, in actuality, it will probably be at least a week before he wakes up, but he is definitely improving."

My family talked about starting a betting pool to see who

could predict when I'd return to consciousness.

A gastroenterologist was called in because of my sluggish liver. But he relieved everyone's worries when he said, "His liver was shocked from all the trauma his body has experienced, and it will most likely be the final organ to recover. I'm not too concerned, but I will adjust his feeding, and I'll monitor his medications for impact on liver function."

Scott, Mark, Julie, and Linda, along with my brother Joe, and his wife, Laurie who were visiting, celebrated the coming of Christmas by catching up on the first few days of Advent. Linda later told me the passages and messages held special meaning that year.

Christmas Eve, Linda's sister, Donna, and Laurie Baumann, came and stayed with me so my wife could spend a few days at home with our kids. I was glad she could take the break.

When she returned, Linda also enjoyed some special "hospital entertainment," when TC Diamond, the needle guy, stopped by and crooned a few Elvis Presley renditions and Christmas songs. He sang, "I Can't Help Falling in Love, White Christmas, and Blue Christmas." She loved it.

A big event happened when doctors were adjusting my pacemaker because my upper chamber was beating too fast. They all thought I'd blinked while they were in the room — something so small, and yet life-changing.

That same night, Linda and Scott saw new signs that I might be regaining consciousness. The washcloth over my eyes moved, causing them to look at each other in disbelief.

Linda said to our son, "Did your dad just blink?"

Scott began talking to me and realized my blood pressure dropped. He experimented with what he said several times, and each time my pressure changed. He asked Linda, "Is it possible? Can he hear us?"

By 8:00 p.m., I blinked and swallowed. I was also responding to my family's voices, and my eyes were beginning to show responsiveness.

On the morning of day twelve, the nurse said I was responding to questions with blinks; once for yes, and twice for no. By that night, I was raising my eyebrows when my family talked about the LSU-GA football game on TV. They said I seemed to look at them when they talked to me — a first since my surgery.

On the fourteenth day, I could focus on faces and responded by blinking and moving my head. As Laurie was holding my feet, she noticed I moved my toes. Everyone gathered around as if new life were coming into the world. When I moved my toes again, they cheered. "You are amazing. We are so proud of you."

Nurse Mary leaned over my bed and asked, "Will you do more tricks for us at the 2:00 p.m. visit?"

Apparently, I shook my head, "Yes," which resulted in more cheers.

I delivered.

I squeezed Dr. Mauney's hand and moved my toes when he examined me, plus I tried to smile at jokes during his afternoon visit. Things seemed to be on an upward trajectory — but then again, sometimes looks are deceiving.

By day fifteen, I was trying to mouth, "I love you," to Linda. My eyes were brighter, and my brows were "speaking" in response to things people said and asked. But my liver scan wasn't good.

They put a tracheotomy in, and things went well. Everyone was surprised when I woke up so soon after the procedure. I shocked them even more when I sat up in bed and began to really look around. I tried to talk, shook my head, smiled, and even tried to laugh when I was told my brother Joe and I needed to go get pedicures together upon my release. They said I winked at Julie on that one.

Dr. Mauney visited and gave me my first verbal report. "It's now been two weeks since your surgery. You had a much more complicated procedure than what we planned — you experienced both heart and kidney failure. But you are also a very tough man. Actually, I'd call you a miracle patient. You have a long recovery ahead of you, and you'll have to work hard, but as time passes, things will get easier.

This afternoon, they'll take you off the slow, continuous dialysis you've been on, and place you on the more powerful, quicker procedure. It will remove your extra fluids at an accelerated rate, and you will only have to do it once per day. You'll also get a new trach in a few days. That should make it easier for you to breathe."

That word, "should," can sometimes get sticky, especially after an extended period where things appear to be getting better.

It was my thirty-sixth day in ICU when Scott and Linda were told I couldn't handle the vent and was having trouble breathing. After a chest x-ray, they discovered more fluid in my lungs. Once they gave me dialysis and pulled more fluids off my body, I improved enough to communicate. I motioned with my hands that I wanted Scott to stay for a while — even though I was obviously worn out. Maybe I was scared, I can't say for sure since I don't remember anything from that time.

By my forty-fourth day, the new year had come and gone. It was January 4, 2012. The big celebration for me was that I could finally feed myself some food — plus it was moving day. I left ICU and headed for my new home, Room 1251. I shocked everyone when I walked past my waiting wheel chair unassisted out of the ICU doors, making it a few more steps, until I collapsed from exhaustion and had to sit down.

My fiftieth day in the hospital brought more progress. My feeding tube and trach were removed, I was going to physical therapy, and I could talk, though my voice was very raspy. One of the first things I wanted to know was if people back home thought I was dead. I don't remember the answer they gave me.

For the first time since I was admitted, I called my brothers, Joe and John, on the telephone. I think they were pretty happy to hear from me. A few days later, John came and stayed through the weekend so Linda could get some much needed rest. I can't imagine going through something like this without strong family and friend support — we were graced with both.

In my final days at Missouri Baptist, I experienced my own roller coaster — one wrought anxiety. Thankfully, I can't recall much of it, at least while I was in the hospital.

Though bacteria still showed up in some of my cultures, and the medical team was perplexed as to the origin of my infection, on January 21, 2012, I was finally released. It was homecoming day!

Our three children came to assist Linda and me. The morning was bittersweet as several doctors came with final instructions and goodbyes. After sixty-one days of what felt like hell together, it was like leaving family.

When they wheeled me down the corridor, a line of white coats, scrubs, and other stethoscope ringed staff, cheered me on. Many of the nurses took pictures as I rolled by. Through loud hand-clapping, a few voices shouted encouragement.

"Way to go."

"We're proud of you, Miracle Man."

"You've got this."

When we pulled into Steelville, a plethora of welcome home and well wishes signs were posted around town. I cried more than once.

At the beginning of my recovery period, I was told I'd be in a wheel chair the rest of my life — if I survived. Though I remember little of my sixty-one days in earthly hell, I do recall one prevailing thing.

A determination to prove them wrong dominated my attitude and pushed me through torment I didn't know the human body could endure. An inner voice kept reminding me to exercise faith in God and His ability to do the impossible. I believe it was the voice of God's Spirit encouraging me when I was too weak to communicate.

I was released from Missouri Baptist exactly ten years to the day from my first heart surgery. In the euphoria of that moment, I believed the worst was behind me. But sometimes the torture in our minds is greater than any pain that racks our bodies. My suffering was far from over.

ROMANS 8:18 (ESV)
"For I consider that the sufferings of this present time are not worth comparing with the glory that is to be revealed to us."

CHAPTER TWELVE

Giving Up

Though I had come a long way, I wasn't completely restored, mentally or physically, when they released me from
the hospital. I needed ongoing treatment for edema, the medical term for swelling in the body, and an infection that doctors were still struggling to pinpoint. Repeatedly, the source
perplexed them.

The first few weeks after I arrived home, I was too weak for
travel. So a health therapist came to the house. Not only did
I get regular doses of professional workouts, but my friends,
Alan Vickers and Loyal Kaeding, came a few times a week to
assist as well.

Alan's good humor took my mind off of my problems. Loyal
had had heart issues of his own. So through experience, he often understood exactly what I needed — even when I didn't
know myself. They made a great caregiving support team.

Eventually, they helped me get strong enough to see Mike
Whittaker for therapy through Missouri Baptist Hospital's rehab facility in Sullivan. Mike was incredible, and his therapeu-

tic exercises helped, though he could never rid me entirely of the floating pain that haunted my body.

My general practitioner, Dr. Modad, along with the medical team in St. Louis, tried numerous treatments to abate the mysterious infection. But as soon as I finished each round of meds, the fever and bone-deep ache returned. A dark depression settled into my soul — I was losing hope.

I hit the hard slate bottom of despair in the summer of 2012. Linda must have noticed too, because she had gathered all of my guns and ammunition, removing them from their safes. I didn't know where she hid them, but I began to obsess about the possibilities. I was in trouble.

I looked at the clock on the wall. My son, Scott, would be playing in a men's golf league at that time. So I called him from my cell.

He answered before the second ring finished. "Hey Dad, what's up?"

"You need to get over here as soon as possible."

"Why? Are you okay?"

"No, I'm not son. I need you to hurry."

I could hear Scott begin to run, his heavy footsteps thudding against pavement as I ended the call.

By the time Scott rushed through the front door, Linda pleaded. "I don't know what to do for you. How can I help you?"

All I could do was repeat the same thing over and over. "I can't take this anymore. I'm done. I can't take it. I can't do this. It's too hard." I never used the term suicide or specifically said I wanted to take my own life, but my wife and son knew exactly what I meant.

Scott comforted his mom, gave her a quick hug, and said, "It's going to be okay, Mom. Why don't you go in the other room and pull yourself together. Let me talk to Dad alone."

Linda sniffled and gave me a desperate look before she followed Scott's instructions.

My son got straight to the point. "What are you thinking? You are not this kind of person. You don't want to disappoint your grandchildren. You don't want to let down all the people who've devoted themselves to you in support and prayer — the ones who've helped our family during this tough time."

I considered what Scott was saying for a couple of minutes. I shook my head in back and forth negative movements, then said, "No. I'd feel bad if I let everyone down."

"Then you can't seriously think about what you're thinking about."

Images of my grandchildren flashed in my mind, along with the faces of friends and co-workers, "I guess you're right."

"I know I am. Now stop this nonsense, and put your fight back on. We need you."

Scott stayed for a long time. After he thought I was past the crisis, and his mother was calm enough to handle me, he finally left to see his own wife and kids. After he went home, I thought about the things he said, and it helped ease my mind. For a while.

What is it about nightime that causes the human condition to worsen? My fever began to spike as the long shadows of evening smothered the day's light. Shifting bouts of chills and burning sensations shook my body. I felt a filmy sweat break out in spots above my upper lip. And the pain that never quite went away intensified into a scorching inferno.

I called out to God. Then I called for my wife. "Linda, it hurts so bad. I can't take this."

"What can I do?"

"Make it stop."

"I would if it were possible, believe me, I would."

"I can't go on like this, Linda. I can't take it anymore. I don't think I'll ever feel good again, I'm ready to give up."

Tears poured off my wife's face and melted into our carpet.

Seeing her so distraught made me even more resolved to do what I was considering. She'd be better off without me.

I decided I'd rather go on my own terms than to suffer and wait, watching the fear and pity escalate in my family's faces. I didn't want to die as much as I wanted the pain to go away. I wanted the peace I'd already experienced in Heaven.

I believed my family would be better off without me and could go on with life, free from the prison of my need for constant care. The way I saw it, I was a burden.

In that moment, I feared living more than I feared death. I decided to take my own life — and I knew exactly how I would do it.

But my wife stood in the way.

I told her, "I'm tired."

"I know you are, but I need you to hang on."

"Where are my guns."

"You don't need them."

"They're my guns."

"And I'm your wife. I need you to be strong for me."

"I can't."

Linda's face was set like iron. "I don't know what to tell you. Call one of your friends, but I'm not going to make this easy for you."

So I did exactly what she suggested — I phoned a friend.

Kem Schweider and I go back to childhood. He's a guy I can call on day or night. We've laughed until our sides stitched, and he knows me better than some of my family. So his reaction to my phone call shouldn't have surprised me.

He answered within a couple of rings. "Hey, Perkins."

"I need a favor, buddy."

"Sure, anything I can do."

"I need a gun. I can't take it anymore. I'm ready to call it quits."

I don't remember if I expected sympathy or alarm. But either way, my friend did not offer the expected.

Kem replied right away. "What caliber of pistol do you want to use?"

His question threw me off. "I'm, I'm not real sure. I, uh, well, I uh, don't guess it matters."

Without missing a breath, Kem said, "Well, I need to know what kind of gun you want so I know what bullets to bring."

I lost it.

Somehow his crazy response burrowed its way to my funny bone, and I began to laugh. A light chuckle at first. Then a cackle, until it soon mushroomed into a belly buster. Kem had hit me with an insider's sense of humor that comes from years of relationship — when you've seen each other at your worst. When you know whether the moment calls for compassion or comedy. At my darkest hour, my pal knew I needed to laugh and how to draw it out of me.

I had forgotten how healing laughter's release feels in my soul. My friend's unexpected response triggered hidden joy in the midst of my bleak circumstances.

Once the laughter echoed away, Kem began to speak in all earnestness. He told me how important I was to my family, to him, to our community, and to others. But he was smart enough to know that before he could speak to me seriously, he'd have to earn my trust.

Kem's humorous spark momentarily snapped me out of my sorrow. It helped me hear him. I realized that as much as my death might bring me peace, it would leave my family in despair. What I previously viewed as an easy escape, would in actuality result in intense sorrow. I decided I could not do that to them. My life wasn't solely about me, but my welfare was important to the people who cared about me.

Another thing that helped me get through that dark season, was my new puppy, Yadi. Named after the great St. Louis Cardinals catcher, Yadier Molina. His unconditional love, plus the purpose provided by caring for his practical needs, gave me a reason to get out of bed each day. Many dark days were lightened by his bright eyes and shining spirit — proof he needed me too.

Though I experienced other depressive periods, never again was suicide an option I considered. The devil might growl in my ear, using his negative language to distract me for a few seconds, but I determined never again to let him have the upper hand.

Instead of listening to his lies, I chose instead to believe the voice of God, speaking hope and encouragement into my life and lifting me above my emotions. God wasn't finished with me yet. A great purpose would result from overcoming my illness.

Developing a positive attitude is a decision I don't regret, and one that my doctors say helped save my life. For a time, I couldn't produce it on my own, I needed the rescuing arm of a friend who didn't shy away from my pain. But who reached into my despair and helped pull me through the dark days.

I wish I could say everything turned rosy once I determined suicide was not a consideration — but unfortunately, my physical pain wouldn't let me escape mental anguish. Incoherence, long-term disability, and near-death would soon knock on my door again.

JEREMIAH 33:3 (NLT)
"Ask me and I will tell you remarkable secrets
you do not know about things to come."

CHAPTER THIRTEEN

Rehab and Gratitude

By October of 2012, I was desperate to make the chronic pain, now settled in my back, go away. Mike Whittaker continued to try various exercises at the Missouri Baptist facility, and I hired a local massage therapist to come to my house.

As the shortening hours of Indian summer waned, I hoped Diane Englesdorfer's magic fingers would numb my throbbing back. On that last evening, I had no idea what would happen when I lay down on the massage table.

Instead of the normal relief I felt when Diane worked on me, the pain didn't budge. The longer she gently kneaded, the more my lower back spasmed and pulsated in fiery barbs that bored deep into my muscles.

I tried to hide my discomfort from her. But in short order, my groans threatened to turn into tears. "I think you'd better stop. I need to get up."

"Of course." Diane pulled her fingers from my skin.

I tried to sit up, but a piercing jab made me freeze in place.

"Can you help me?" I pleaded.

Diane positioned herself to best support my 6'4" frame. On a three count, she tried to help me hoist myself off the massage table. A hard stab in the sinews of my back made me yell. "Stop. Wait. Not yet."

Diane obeyed instantly.

It took a bit for me to catch my breath and allow my heart palpitations to subside. When they did, Diane set up to try again. But the same thing happened.

She waited patiently for my body to rest, and my mind to allow another attempt. A few minutes later, soft footsteps padded toward the table.

I was relieved to hear Linda's voice. "Is everything okay?"

"Not really," I said.

"Can I help?"

Diane said, "How about if you stand over here, and we'll try to ease him up together. I'll move to the other side of the table." Diane walked around, and changed to a light pushing motion instead of the easy tug she tried before. "Okay, I'm ready. One. Two. Three. Humph."

I yelped. "Stop. Stop. Stop. I'm sorry. I can't handle this way either."

Diane helped me fall back under her supportive hands. "Don't worry about it. We'll get you there."

"I sure hope so," my words came through ragged breaths. "Let me rest for a few minutes, and we can try again."

"I'm in no hurry. Take your time." Diane comforted.

Linda stroked my arm and shoulder in soothing butterfly brushes.

While I concentrated on slowing my inhales and exhales, I glanced out the window across the room. The shadows of evening had been replaced with night's darkness. "What time is it?"

"After nine," Linda said.

I took a deep breath. "I'm ready."

"You sure?" Diane said.

"No, but I have to try."

"Okay." Diane arranged she and Linda to get the most out of their combined efforts. "On the count of three again. One. Two. Three."

They moved me about two inches before I screamed. "It's no use. I think you're going to have to call an ambulance."

By the time the EMT's loaded me up for transport to Missouri Baptist Hospital in St. Louis, it was after 10:00 p.m. I have no idea how late it was when the ambulance arrived at the emergency room, but the ER crew quickly admitted me, hooked me up to an IV and monitoring equipment, asked Linda and me a litany of questions, and started tests. It seemed like days before they were able to administer enough pain meds to take the edge off. The strength and dosage knocked me out.

The test results finally came back. It showed I had a severe case of staph infection originating from an unknown source that had radiated into my back. I hurt so badly — I could no longer get out of a bed.

Immediately, they began a round of powerful antibiotics while they tried to find the source. The merry-go-round was about to begin.

For several days my condition worsened, improving when the antibiotics infiltrated my system. Then it worsened again as soon as my doctors tried to wean me off. To make things more difficult, the level of pain medications my body required made me feel groggy and lethargic. It didn't take long for my insurance company to deny benefits for me to stay in the hospital. Instead, they wanted me to enter a rehab center in St. Louis for long-term treatment. I did not want to be that far from home.

Thankfully, my family was able to arrange long-term rehabilitation at Gibbs Care Center, a skilled nursing facility in

Steelville with a therapy center. I would stay indefinitely, until my body and mind developed enough strength to manage living at home.

I hated feeling helpless.

I learned some things about myself as I endured. My son, Mark, was not afraid to tell me I was a very tough coach and a very tough dad, especially on him since he's the oldest.

I was a hands-on father. I pushed discipline and believed you had to keep going until you completed what you started. I worked side by side with my children, from mowing the lawn to hauling hay on the farm. But I also played side by side with them. I coached them when they were young in basketball. And I admit, I was a perfectionist — and not just about the game.

I required neat surroundings and orderly living. I allowed nothing left laying around in boxes or on counters, I wanted everything put away in its place.

I believe the discipline I learned and passed on to my kids helps them as adults. But during my rehab period, the tables turned. Suddenly, my kids were repeating what I had taught them earlier.

I remember few of my days as a patient at Gibbs Care Center — but what I do recall is a mixture of seriousness and funny moments. While it was happening, I don't think I liked any of it.

According to my wife and kids, when I was in Gibbs, I sat slouched over, head hanging to my chest for hours, without moving or making a sound. One day, Mark and Linda were talking quietly, and began to laugh.

They said I suddenly snapped my head up without warning and said, "Why are you laughing at me? I can't believe you're making fun of me. This isn't funny."

After the shock of my outburst subsided, my wife and son walked out into the hall and ignored my continued ranting.

They weren't laughing at me anyway.

My chin lowered, and I resumed my new normal position. I have no memory of that encounter.

According to Mark, another humorous episode occurred after I could brush my teeth on my own. Mark squeezed toothpaste onto my brush and moistened the bristles. I began brushing my teeth.

Ten minutes later, I was still brushing.

Mark said, "Hey Dad, I think your teeth should be clean now."

I shot back, "Not yet."

Fifteen minutes passed. Mark questioned me again, "Don't you think your teeth are clean?"

I told him, "No."

Twenty minutes later, he dared to bring up the subject again. "Your teeth have got to be clean."

"No," I said again.

Finally, after twenty-five solid minutes of brushing, Mark went over and grabbed the brush, and said, "Dad, your teeth are clean. Let's put things up and get you in bed."

I would have made any dentist proud that night.

My daughter, Julie, said one time when she was there I began talking nonsense. I said, "Is everything ready for the party?"

She asked, "What party?"

I didn't answer.

Only God knows what party I meant.

Julie said they never knew whether it was okay to ask me, "How are you?"

Often I gave a one word answer. "Rough."

According to all who dared visit me during that dark period, I wasn't myself. Some described me as being in a perpetual state of suffering.

I distanced myself from people, including my grandkids

who I adore. No one could do anything right for me during my rehabilitation at the nursing home. When I was sick, I would bark at my boys for trying to help me. Julie walked on eggshells. Linda was worn down from taking care of me, as well as dealing with her own health issues.

When you are chronically ill, and your body is in a constant condition of unrest, pain, and discomfort, it's almost impossible to behave nicely — you truly are not yourself. When you don't feel good, you don't act good.

If the caregiver(s) can remember they are dealing with the disease or other traumatic event overtaking your physical being, it can help them survive your cranky, grumpy, and even verbally abusive outbursts. Thankfully, my family did that for me.

If my family and the staff at Gibbs Care Center hadn't taken care of me, I probably wouldn't be telling you my story now. They protected me from dangerous falls, pushed me to strengthen my body when I hit the brick wall and wanted to give up, and pulled me from the brink several times when I had other close calls. But it wasn't just the big rescues that mattered — they also saved me in the daily details — helping me do little things until I was capable of handling them on my own. And dealing with my grouchy attitude all the while.

Here's a fact about being disabled — once your right mind begins to return, you discover how much you take for granted. Getting up and using the bathroom on your own. Sneezing without it causing sharp pains. The ability to put your toothpaste on your toothbrush. Having the stamina to stand under a hot shower. I now appreciate all of these things, whereas I didn't give them much thought before.

Though I loved my family before my illness, I didn't always tell them. I thought mental toughness and a constant focus on discipline were the best ways to demonstrate my care for them. Now I realize it's okay to show my sensitivity. I'm no longer afraid to let my family see my emotions. My wife's disposition provides benefits, allowing softness to display her inner strength. I'm learning from her. I was acting out of fear when I displayed tough-mindedness.

There is a domino effect when a family member is struck with a serious illness. It impacts everyone — the person who's sick, the spouse, children, the children's spouses, and grandchildren, aunts, uncles, cousins, and others. However, if we choose a teachable attitude, the results become positive.

There's nothing wrong with discipline, mental toughness, order, or other serious pursuits. They are good for you — in balance. But it's equally healthy and vitally important to relax, laugh, let your guard down, and demonstrate love in words and actions.

The old me still surfaces, such as the day I surprised Mark and Linda with my outburst in the nursing home, making ridiculous accusations. The difference now is my willingness to acknowledge my mistakes and my desire to show my sincere regret when I hurt someone.

As a committed follower of Jesus Christ, I cannot imitate him perfectly while I'm still in this body. But I can continue striving to match his perfect balance. It might be possible to overbrush my teeth, but I doubt I can do that to my soul.

I'd like to say when they finally released me from rehab at Gibbs that my life improved, however, this wasn't my experience. I couldn't regain my energy, I still felt very weak and sick. And the doctors couldn't tell me why.

Deep in my spirit, I longed for the freedom I'd felt during my death experience. It wasn't something I talked about, but I thought about it obsessively during those dark days. I often felt like giving up, but I reminded myself that I was still alive for a reason. It was up to me to push through and to find out why.

I think the doctors were as mentally exhausted as I was, baffled by my ongoing infections. They finally released me to go home. But I'd soon be in the hospital again.

PSALM 119:75 (NLT)
"I know, O Lord, that your regulations are fair;
you disciplined me because I needed it."

CHAPTER FOURTEEN

A Grim Prognosis

In late spring of 2013, my general practitioner, Dr. Modad, was frustrated. No matter what he or any of my other physicians tried, they couldn't get rid of the infection ravaging me on the inside. So, he picked up his phone and dialed the number in front of him.

Within a couple of rings, a secretary answered, "Dr. Hayes's office, may I help you?"

"This is Dr. Modad, from Cuba, Missouri, Dr. Hayes's hometown, I was wondering if I might speak with him."

"He's in a meeting at the moment, may I have him call you back?"

"That would be fine. Thank you."

Dr. Hayes returned the call promptly.

"How can I help you, Dr. Modad?"

"I'd like to talk with you about one of my patients and see if I can arrange a referral to Mayo. We've exhausted our efforts here in Missouri. And this man needs help quickly."

Things moved fast. Dr. Modad had me sign a release so Dr.

Hayes could access my medical records. Dr. Modad arranged everything.

By early summer, Linda and I were on a plane chartered by our good friend, Kem Schwieder, flying us to Rochester, Minnesota. But the trip was hard on me.

I had to recline in the back of the small plane. But because I'm so tall, I couldn't extend my legs fully. Scott sat in the co-pilot's seat, while Linda sat next to me, soothing me when I cried or laid my head on her shoulder. This is not easy for a grown, self-reliant man to confess.

Though the pilot flew at low elevation to reduce the pressure on my body, the flight still magnified the pain caused from inflammation due to staph. The ride was long in endurance compared to the short time it actually took.

When we arrived at Mayo, a battery of early tests and an initial consult revealed how seriously ill I was. Immediately, I became a patient in the Mayo Clinic system.

I saw one of the top cardiologists at the Mayo Clinic. Interestingly, he hailed from our area of Missouri.

The expanse of the Mayo Clinic is vast in downtown Rochester. Sprawling medical complexes cover numerous city blocks, with multiple offices specializing in every aspect of human health.

Dr. Hayes' office looked much like many others in the area — nondescript, a couple of floors up, overlooking squared central heat and air units next to round air circulators spinning their silver cylinders. The interior of his office was surprisingly small, tidy, with a row of organizational compartments and a couple of shelves housing books relating to heart issues.

Dr. Hayes's expression embodied kindness. And the warmth of his voice reinforced what I read in his body language. Light brown hair, with trace amounts of silver, framed thin facial features and sparkling, almond-shaped eyes. He appeared fit, although not overtly muscled. I towered him in height, probably by at least six inches. But I still felt diminutive in his presence. He was the opposite of arrogant. Yet as he seated us, I could tell I was sitting across from a great man.

I was nervous. Yet for the first time in recent memory, I felt real hope. I didn't know Dr. Hayes, but I knew his family by reputation. We had grown up eight miles apart. And in our area, the shoe store his family founded decades ago is still known for its quality goods and reasonable prices. People travel many miles to buy from Hayes Shoe Store. My family regularly bought our shoes from his family's business.

When I met with Dr. Hayes, I felt strangely comfortable as I learned more about him.

From the time he was a child, for no particular reason he can remember, David Hayes wanted to work in medicine. According to his mother, he began to talk about it as young as age six.

When he was a young man in high school, he set his sights on medical school and applied for the first formal six year medical program offered at University of Missouri, Kansas City. As destiny would have it, he was accepted. The very first week, he had direct interactions with patients in a hospital setting. And he was hooked. This was what he wanted to do with his life. In a class of forty, he thrived.

David quickly mastered the basics he would need as a medical administrator when he worked in his family's shoe store. It was the foundation on which he would build a highly successful medical career. Like myself, his life seemed to have been laid out for him.

He said, "What I learned about working with patients wasn't taught in medical school textbooks or lectures — I gleaned it from real life experience."

What some might see as a meager beginning, selling shoes in the family business taught him how to deal with people.

In the medical field, whether interacting with patients, colleagues, a staff member who reports to you, another physician, boards, or those in leadership, it's all about relationships. Treating people with respect. Listening. The appropriateness of what to say and what not to say. How to be honest with people, while simultaneously demonstrating compassion.

He showed one way his background taught him the importance of detail and clear communication skills. He said, "As a boy, I was trained to determine whether a shoe would stretch with wear or to know if a particular style ran small. It was up to me to make sure my customers truly heard and understood what I needed to tell them. Clear communication was my responsibility, not theirs. I owe my patients the same clarity."

He continued, "Never underestimate the value of what you learn in the everyday from ordinary people. It can change your life in ways you won't imagine until you realize it later."

I thought of my parents and grandparents, then I nodded.

David smiled, "I'm naturally analytical. I've learned what you are made for doesn't always make itself blatantly obvious. Instead, as in my case, I had to check off the things I didn't want to do, until I narrowed the data down. I started the process when I was pretty young, before I really knew what I was doing. But it helped me discover my true passion lying at the bottom."

His approach was fascinating. But I still didn't know how a guy from Cuba, Missouri, ended up as one of the top cardiologists in the nation, working at one of the world's best hospitals. "Was it your goal to work at Mayo?"

He smiled as if he were reliving a happy moment. "Actually, some unusual events brought me here. I ended up finishing my time at UMKC early and I began interviewing for residencies off schedule."

He explained, "It was early summer, and I flew from Kansas City to Chicago and interviewed at the University of Chicago.

I knew immediately it wasn't the place for me, so from Chicago I flew straight to Rochester so I could interview for a position at Mayo that was slated to begin in January."

He grinned wide, "This was over thirty years ago, and the airport was so small my plane literally landed on a strip between two cornfields. The hospital was built in the middle of nowhere. And yet, I knew, this was it — I was meant to work at Mayo."

He added, "My wife's a cardiologist here, too. And we still believe this is where we belong. The pieces of my life fell into place as they were meant to. That's my story."

I couldn't help thinking his tale was one more example of the providential pieces woven together that were affecting my own life. I think God knew I would need Dr. Hayes's expertise. And as I sat across from him, I was very grateful to hear it.

"From what I can see in your records, you have advanced heart disease with secondary pulmonary issues. Further complicating things is this ongoing fever and infection you've not been able to get passed."

"But I will. There's a whole lot of people praying for me," I assured him.

"That's good. I'm glad you're an optimist. I have an idea of what might be causing your repeated episodes of sepsis. But let me examine you. Then I'd like to consult with a couple of my colleagues. In particular, I want to speak with an infectious disease specialist on staff, along with a panel of other physicians."

He continued, "Ultimately, I'm probably going to refer you to Dr. Borgeson. As much as optimism is important, so is realism. Heart failure is his specialty, and I believe his opinion is critical to your care. My area of expertise is heart devices. Things like pacemakers, defibrillators, valves, and resynchronization devices."

Since I'm a jokester by nature, I thought about making

a wisecrack. But I could tell this wasn't the time. Besides, I wasn't feeling so great. So instead, I nodded my head in agreement and said, "Whatever you suggest, you're the expert."

He smiled, made some notes, and ordered some tests. Then, he told me he would be in touch soon. I went back to Missouri, and I waited as the Mayo team evaluated my case. A few weeks later, they called me to come back.

Dr. Hayes and the group of physicians he consulted with all agreed — I had a serious case of staph infection. As I was told later, the infectious disease specialist told Dr. Hayes, "Wow, this is a really complicated case."

I also found out that Dr. Hayes thought my prognosis was grim. Dr. Hayes was not optimistic from a medical perspective. However, he never let on. But I do understand why he thought that way.

In addition to advanced stage heart disease and the secondary pulmonary issues, Dr. Hayes said he also believed staph infection was hiding in a cavity around my previously implanted heart hardware. Unless my pacemaker was removed, with the multiplicity of other complications, my quality of life was very poor and might not improve much. In his qualified opinion, a left ventricular/assist device or transplant team were needed more than anything than he could offer. But even those weren't options until they had the staph infection under control.

When hardware is placed inside the human body and staph attaches itself to the hardware, there isn't much you can do except remove the hardware. If a person does not have hardware in their body and gets staph, it can be treated with antibiotics. But hardware cannot be disinfected, so it must be removed. Dr. Hayes said I needed a procedure to extract my heart hardware — not a small matter.

I was scheduled for surgery right away. In Dr. Hayes medical opinion, if he hadn't removed my heart hardware, I would have repeatedly experienced episodes of sepsis, potentially lethal bacteria and toxins rooted in a wound or infection — in my case it was staph. But the extraction of my hardware was not an easy task.

There were multiple wires going through major veins into the right side and upper chamber of my heart. In Dr. Hayes' words, "It was a tricky procedure."

Adding to the challenges, scar tissue had grown over the intricate pieces of hardware and around the leads into my blood vessels. The scar tissue had to be moved away in order to extract the lead from the vein in my heart. Too much tug would have created a rip in the tissues of the vein or heart, leading to a lethal outcome for me. The odds were in my favor. Approximately 98% of the time, when these procedures are done at Mayo they are successful in removing all of the infected hardware with a 1% or less risk for death.

In a typical case, they open up the chest cavity, expose the wires, cut off the bulbous ends, take a laser, and one wire at a time, burn away the scar tissue from around the lead. The physician must finesse the process, gently pulling on the lead wire, while simultaneously lasering the tissue, keeping just the right amount of tension at play. At times, the right ventricle may invert, because the lead is pulling pretty hard. In a best-case scenario, as the doctor gets down to the last wire, the last little piece of scar tissue gives way, popping out and releasing the lead. Only then can the cardiologist take a moment to exhale a full breath and allow his adrenalin to dissipate.

There's no predicting a time for this delicate procedure. It depends on how many wires are involved and how much the scar tissue has grown. In some cases it's a quick release, while others are a battle.

Thankfully, Dr. Hayes performed mine without incident. And in doing so, he found a pocket of staph attached to my device. However, I wasn't out of the woods.

Though the immediate danger of staph infection was addressed, and it was determined I was at no immediate risk without my pacemaker, heart failure quickly ensued. No amount of hardware could fix this.

Upon my release, I was sent home for a longer recovery, so my body could recuperate for a referral meeting with Dr. Dan Borgeson. Dr. Hayes wasn't sure how things would progress for me from that point.

I went home to wait on the next step.

In August of 2013, I was strong enough for my return to Rochester — though I was still very weak. Dr. Borgeson wanted to see me as soon as possible. We decided to try driving, though my pain level hadn't eased in the weeks since my first visit to the Mayo Clinic.

While we traversed the miles by car, Linda, our daughter, Julie, and Linda's three sisters, kept their plans for a quick getaway to Chicago — something they'd scheduled previous to my call to Mayo. I didn't want to disappoint them, so after much discussion, they made their trip. Linda would catch a flight from Chicago to Rochester, while the rest of the getaway group returned to St. Louis.

Mark and Scott would chauffeur me, so we decided to take Linda's Cadillac Escalade. My sons removed the back seats, blew up a large camping air mattress, and eased me onto it for the nine hour drive. It was uncomfortable, but I was used to discomfort by then. It was my new way of life.

Bathroom and eating stops were the worst. Mark and Scott had to help me roll off and on my mattress. I probably looked like a clumsy giraffe trying to get off the ground, with my long body getting in my own way. But eventually we made it to Dr. Borgeson's office.

He was gentle with his words, though his message was serious. "You may not qualify for transplant, since you are nearing the age limit, plus other health issues at play must be overcome first."

I was at the beginning of my education about the organ transplant process. My first lesson?

Regardless of some people's assumptions, neither fortune nor fame can buy you an organ transplant in the United States. Health is one of those elusive things that money cannot buy. Mine was diminishing at a rapid rate. My heart wasn't the only thing failing — my kidneys were nearing their end as well.

PSALM 38:7 (NIV)
"My back is filled with searing pain;
there is no health in my body."

CHAPTER FIFTEEN

Treating with Transplant

The staff at the Mayo Clinic in Rochester was impressive beyond their skills — the attitude with which they treated me as their patient was world class. The physician who probably worked with me the most was Dr. Borgeson, a cardiologist specializing in heart failure.

I liked him immediately — he's a rare man, mixing high intelligence with down-to-earth common sense. I've met very few men with his depth of wisdom. My loyalty was guaranteed when he said, "I don't believe in average care for average patients for average results."

Dr. Borgeson was very open with his personal philosophies from the start, sharing that he strives to become friends with his patients, knowing the importance of relationship when it comes to quality of healthcare. If he perceives a patient can handle it, he even uses quirky medical humor to relax tensions. I think he quickly understood my needs and personality.

He teased me early on, "You don't get extra points for dying with normal lab values." He added, "And I have to tell you, it doesn't do you any good to fix the thing you died from second."

This might bother some folks, but it put me at ease. I have a quirky sense of humor myself, so I appreciated the laughter.

On a more serious note, Dr. Borgeson believes, "Physicians should try to find something unrelated to health to connect with their patients about. To create a personal bond of some kind, so they can identify with each other. This improves communication, reduces tension, builds trust, and improves efficiency in treating a condition."

I agreed 100%. I wanted a doctor my family could talk to.

Dr. Borgeson has an interesting life story. He never planned on becoming a doctor. He grew up on a small farm in North Dakota, where there were only eight males in his upper three grades of high school, located in a little dinky town where he missed a single room school house by only four years. The nearest McDonald's was seventy-five miles away.

He went to college, then on to pharmacy school. In his last year of rotation in pharmacy school, he visited a Veterans Administration facility and rounded with physicians. It was then he knew he would pursue medicine.

He chuckled when he said, "If you would have told my classmates in high school I'd be a cardiologist, they would have laughed. Sometimes life turns out so much differently than we thought it would. Life happens to you and you have to be ready for it — to grab opportunities when they present themselves. Your occupation chooses you as much as you choose it. You have to persist in moving ahead with something until you discover what you are meant to do. By then you should be practiced in persistence, which will serve you well in transforming dreams into reality. We must be willing to delay and sacrifice if that's what it takes to fulfill our intended destiny."

I told you he was a wise man.

My time under Dr. Borgeson's care reinforced much of what I had learned through my own experiences. I only wish I'd known him when I was younger, because he might have prevented costly mistakes with family, friends, and colleagues.

After I'd seen him a few times, and we were both comfortable with each other, we somehow got into a particularly philosophical conversation. He told me, "The most dangerous people I meet are those who believe they already know everything. They aren't teachable. I've learned to never say never, and never say always."

Amen to that.

He added, "Good health requires the same things as any other successful endeavor. You have to see beyond your own being. Making things all about yourself doesn't work, especially in healthcare. To achieve victory in anything, interact with other people, discover a purpose, focus on things greater than yourself. And seek faith — a foundational belief in something or someone beyond yourself provides stability when things feel shaky. My patients who follow this track ultimately have better outcomes."

I couldn't have stated these truths better myself.

According to Dr. Borgeson, there are two groups of heart failure patients.

One group gets a mechanical assist or a transplant. Sadly the second group does not qualify, or doesn't live long enough for intervention methods. I can't imagine having to make the decisions he and the Mayo teams face on a daily basis, or seeing outcomes for which they cannot control.

Dr. Borgeson told me, "There are only three types of treatments in the world:

1. Things that improve your symptoms.
2. Things that improve your survival.
3. Things you shouldn't do.

When things become really complicated, the best thing

you can do is step back from the situation and evaluate things from this perspective. Ask yourself which treatment makes the most sense."

Dr. Borgeson and his medical team must mentally divide the patients they see. They are required to ask themselves and each other a series of life-altering questions.

"Is this the beginning of the end? Or is it a bump in the road of this patient's life?"

According to Dr. Borgeson, my case was questionable at first. They weren't sure which group I belonged in. But one thing he did later confirm, I was in the tenth percentile of his sickest patients. Yet he said I was one of the most optimistic, ambitious, and tenacious people he'd ever met. I'm glad, because apparently my mental state helped the Mayo team categorize me into the group that would qualify me for transplant consideration.

Dr. Borgeson later told my family about the specifics of my situation.

"Paul's is a very unusual case. Few travel the road to transplant through hypertrophic cardiomyopathy, which is a thick, stiff heart. People with hypertrophic cardiomyopathy have a high-pumping function in their heart, different from most who have a low-pumping function."

He added, "Think of it like this — when you blow air in a balloon, you get high changes in volume with high changes in pressure. But Paul's heart is like blowing into a tin can — with small changes in volume, even though he has high changes in pressure. This makes him appear fairly normal on the outside, though he is very sick on the inside."

He explained, "One of the few noticeable symptoms he experiences is extreme shortness of breath. But even then, especially with his gregarious personality, only family and close friends understand that he feels bad. Until recently, no one knew just how bad his health was — even Paul, himself."

When my wife asked if a change in lifestyle habits would help, Dr. Borgeson was quick to reply. "Paul's illness is not related to his lifestyle, it's purely because of his genetics. He did nothing to create it, and he can do nothing to prevent it. But he does have something special on his side."

He continued, "We rarely see patients with his kind of determined fortitude. It gives a physician a greater degree of confidence that there could be a positive outcome. For those of us who work in medicine, we're human too. And we need to know the patient is fighting as hard as we are. With Paul, I don't question this is the case."

I went from 215 pounds to 179 pounds between August 31, to September 11, in 2013. This was due to fluid they removed at Mayo and the leaks they closed around my heart. My doctors hoped this was enough to stabilize me — but it only worked for about a year before I got sick again.

Dr. Borgeson admitted me to the hospital again, in late September, 2013 to see if it was time for a heart transplant. Though he was compassionate, he was also blunt.

"I feel you might not have more than two years without a transplant, but under no circumstances do I consider replacing organs unless all other alternatives are exhausted. Most people don't realize that when you get a transplant, you trade one disease for another. You must take daily meds, constant precautions are required, and side-effects are regular challenges. This is not something the patient or physician should explore lightly."

Few people understand the formula for quantifying whether someone is a good candidate for heart transplant. Why should they, unless they reach dire conditions, or they are close to a person who does?

Dr. Borgeson broke the process down into laymen's terms my family and I could comprehend.

In our hospital, these factors are measured and/or taken into account before making a recommendation:

1. Identify the existence of a heart problem that cannot be corrected with meds, hardware, or other measures. Determine the patient is sick enough in the heart, but healthy enough in their other organs and the rest of their body.

2. Consider the patient's age. They must be under 70, the cut-off for a heart transplant. Different organs have various age limitations. So for you, because your kidneys are also at risk, I'll need to consult with your nephrologist as well as our transplant team.

3. Determine if there are any other serious organ diseases, such as kidney or liver, but particularly pulmonary lung issues. Pulmonary hypertension, or high blood pressure in the lungs would greatly complicate any potential for transplant. Heart and lung transplants are very difficult.

4. Conduct a hema-endemic cath test to measure the pressures inside the heart. During this procedure a catheter, a thin tube of medical grade material, is inserted into the body in order to draw out fluids for evaluation.

5. Look for social support — ensure there are people who can be there and help the patient during their healing process.

6. Assess the mental makeup of the patient to determine if they have the stamina to endure the physical and emotional effects of a transplant. Mental toughness is crucial in predicting a patient's success post-transplant. They must have the willingness and ability to fight for their own health. This is done through a trained transplant psychologist who analyzes the patient to see if they would handle the emotional and mental impact of a transplant.

Many possible scenarios are discussed. Can the patient handle survivor's guilt over the person who died in order for them to live? Are they willing to see doctors for the rest of their life? Are they willing to deal with the side-effects of post-transplant medications? Are they willing to take their required meds on a daily basis for the rest of their life?

7. Explore patient's potential for close proximity to the medical team after the surgery. They are asked, "Can you be in the area of the hospital for several weeks after the transplant for follow-up?"

Dr. Borgeson explained that this formula allows him to make an informed decision about a course of individual patient care. He said, "It's imperative to avoid distractors that can slow down or prevent a physician from efficiently assisting a patient in their search for better health. A series of questions solidifies the process."

I felt as if I met the criteria Dr. Borgeson listed. As fast as my health was declining, I could only hope the Mayo teams agreed. I wasn't sure how much longer I could continue feeling as badly as I did.

None of this was easy to hear, to feel, or to contemplate. But having physicians I trusted lightened the weight of it. Knowing your doctor is working as hard as you are makes all the difference in how much you dare to hope.

I can tell you from experience, Dr. Borgeson, while all business, is equally all heart. His way of investigating before making a decision is professional and thorough, but also warm and caring.

He explained that he invites each patient into the decision-making strategy through a course of verbal examination where he reviews a series of questions, and discusses his thoughts with his patient.

Dr. Borgeson said, "I ask myself, *Will a medication improve your symptoms, or will this medication improve your odds for survival?* If the answer is no, then another course of action must be considered. You shouldn't be on a drug if it doesn't do one of those."

His common-sense approach helped me understand the why behind what he recommended for my treatment.

After this, Dr. Borgeson asks another question, "Is this *the* problem, or a problem?"

In my case, the driving force behind my health issues was my heart, so he decided a transplant would help solve the problem.

The final questions he considers, "Will this treatment (transplant) help this patient live longer? Will this treatment help this patient feel better, improving their quality of life?"

If the answer is "no," he says you shouldn't do the transplant.

He adds, "When someone puts a challenge before us, we must ask, "Now what do I have to do to solve the problem?"

Another insight Dr. Borgeson shared made a lot of sense.

He said, "Most people, generally speaking, come to the hospital because they want to feel better more than they want to live longer. Immediate relief is at the forefront of their thinking. The challenge is how to keep them maintaining their health from a preventative perspective, when they begin to feel better and tire of the routine necessary to protect them from further harm."

Passion is another reason I respect this man so much.

He told me that in my case, numerous factors were tried and/or considered:

1. Get the fluids off to provide me with immediate relief and to reduce pressure on the already wearied organs in my body.

2. Try to keep the fluids from coming back. Repair the leaks that lead to fluid buildup.

3. Give me an integral observation period to see how I did. He said I did fair, but not that well.

4. When I started to fail, Dr. Borgeson began to look at other options. He told me I wasn't a great surgical candi-

*date for traditional heart procedures. But he did remove
fluid again, and he gave me a higher dosage of water pills
in efforts to keep more fluid from accumulating. The results weren't ideal. After removing 45 pounds of fluid and
plugging leaks, there was some improvement. But I still
had my genetic heart issue, hypertrophic cardiomyopathy.
No medicine or simple procedure was going to repair my
thick heart. No matter what else he tried, my situation
wouldn't change, the problem would still be there.*

*5. He considered if it was time to do something more
novel. He said, "You were right at the window, sick enough
for a transplant, but healthy enough to survive."*

Dr. Borgeson didn't want to wait until I became too sick or
reached an age where transplant was no longer an option. So
that's why he pulled the trigger and put me on the transplant
list in November of 2013.

I was approved and listed as a 1-B transplant patient for
heart and kidney. The only stage above for transplant consideration is a 1-A, which would require hospitalization.

Now all I could do was wait at a distance no further than
four hours away from the hospital. I was medically and mentally ready to go, all I needed were the organs.

But the waiting wasn't easy. Not because of impatience, although I confess it crept into my mind occasionally — but
because of what held me and my family in limbo. How do you
dream of renewing your own life, knowing it will necessitate
someone else's death?

I would have plenty of time to find out. As the calendar
turned on the brutal midwest winter of 2013, flipping into
January of 2014, my wife and I moved temporarily from
Missouri to Minnesota. Many days of anxious anticipation lay
ahead.

Except for God, I dared not allow anyone to know the
thoughts I wrestled with constantly. There were moments I

wondered if my eyes would again view yellow daffodils signaling spring and resurrection. I tried to hide, even from myself, the creeping emotions that accompanied each physical symptom. The worse I felt, the more I feared.

Gray, heavy clouds seemed like premonitions. The Lord and I had a lot to discuss.

PSALM 34:4 (NIV)
"I sought the Lord, and he answered me;
he delivered me from all my fears."

CHAPTER SIXTEEN

Minnesota Nice

Minnesota is a multi-nicknamed state. Tags such as, *Land of Ten Thousand Lakes, State of Hockey, The North Star State,* and *Land of Sky Blue Waters* are some of its more famous monikers. However, from the folks I've met, my favorite is *Minnesota Nice* — so labeled for the courteous, reserved, and mild-mannered dispositions of those born and raised there.

Truly, some of the kindest people on the planet exist in Minnesota — especially those who work at the Mayo Clinic. I would feel the same way about them regardless of how things ultimately turned out with my health. Their hospitality reminds me of my Missouri neighbors. Maybe it's a midwest thing.

I'm fortunate in my circumstances to have a career that enabled me to move close to the Mayo Clinic, before it was too late, while we hoped for a heart and kidney. My sons, Mark and Scott, took over the day-to-day operations of First Community National Bank, FCNB, while my daughter, Julie, ran our FCNB Insurance agency. Linda and I set up house among the nice people of Minnesota; then, we tried to pretend things were somewhat normal.

I concentrated a lot of mental energy on the blessing of having the means to do what many cannot. Yet I still struggled emotionally as well as physically. Again, I felt like Job. Though I didn't lose all my wealth, I did lose my health — and my peace of mind. Money cannot buy serenity.

The kids took turns coming to visit, as did a couple of particularly close friends, including my buddy, Kem Schweider. Their time with us offered a welcome distraction and reprieve from boredom.

I've always been a worker. This created an unforeseen challenge when I didn't have a job to go to each day. A person needs a reason to get out of bed for, and there's not much a sick man can do in Minnesota during the winter. Visits from friends and family are great incentives for healthy movement.

It was football and basketball seasons, so another respite came from games on television. But I still struggled mentally. As my body degenerated, my wife worked hard to keep my spirits from dipping too low. Periodic medical appointments measured my consistent decline. Minnesotans were still nice, but I could feel despair once again seeping into my soul.

We were limited in the range we could travel from the hospital, in case life-saving organs suddenly came available. My own body was imprisoning me, and I'm a man who enjoys his freedom. Plus, the longer we waited, the more tired and ill I felt.

I spent a week in the hospital the last few days of January, until my release on February 3. The doctors had to remove body fluids and take me off of Coumadin temporarily so they could do a right heart cath, going through my neck. Before my release, they placed a PICC line in my body, a semi-permanent IV line so my wife could administer medications at home. At the time, we thought they were to keep my fluids stable, but we found out later their true purpose was to keep my health from declining further.

For most of February, other than follow up blood tests and appointments with the transplant team, we waited. I'm not sure there's a more difficult directive from The Lord than Psalm 46:10: "Be still, and know that I am God!"

I knew who He was. But I must admit, I hated being still. However, He didn't allow me any say in the matter.

My wife made it through February without stringing me up, but only because of her calm, even-keeled demeanor. I'm sure I was miserable to live with while she flushed my lines daily and changed my IV medicine every forty-eight hours.

Thankfully, we got a visit from one of our kids and grand-kids each time Linda was near a breaking point. Otherwise, I might not have survived for the transplant. Even my gentle wife has her limits. Caregivers never get enough credit for all they endure, particularly when days and weeks stretch into months and years.

In the bleak days of winter, when snow piled high in Minnesota and darkness seemed to creep into our spirits, brightness landed in our mailbox and lightened our lives through cards and letters. Unless you've withstood the kind of trauma my body and mind endured, you don't realize how much of a difference someone else can make when they take the time to send a hope-filled message. Never discount the power of encouraging words — many friends helped us get through the difficulty of waiting for my transplant.

My second mom, Edith Becker, sent me a card every month. She was close friends with my mother when she was alive, but Edith continued demonstrating her love by befriending me. From the time I can remember, Edith taught me, "When someone else is down — step up."

Edith stepped up and lifted me above many a depressive moment when her cards came in the mail. I anticipated their arrival, and her consistency gave me something to look forward to.

Between the trickle of notes from other friends, a package arrived on February 12, 2014, from our daughter Julie's friend, Anne Buchanan. Anne is an extended part of our family. She's also a schoolteacher, and her class of seventh graders accepted a challenge to commit random acts of kindness. I was blessed by their inspirational messages, but one really stood out.

A student made a collage of newspaper article clippings, and wrote in black magic marker over the top. "Just because the past didn't turn out how you wanted, doesn't mean the future can't be better than you ever imagined."

Not only do I still have that piece of inspirational art, but it is now framed among other notes from Anne's class, publicly displayed at First Community National Bank in Steelville. The day I received it, I stood outside in the snow holding it for a picture. Barely a month later, a new heart would beat inside my chest. A year later, I would travel to businesses, conferences, and churches passing on a message of hope and encouragement. Less than two years later, the book you hold in your hands would be written. Anne's student was right, my future turned out much better than I could have imagined.

We received another package from our granddaughter Naomi's class in mid-February. Her teacher, Mrs. Dionne Haskell, sent pictures and stories from the children, along with motivating thoughts. Naomi slipped in an 8x10, copied photo of herself, Marli, Emeri, and Adalei, with a note that said, "us sisters."

Several of the students even drew and sent me a "new heart" in case my transplant was delayed. I'm not sure teachers and students who do this kind of thing realize how powerfully their outreaches help a person get through tough days.

Packages and individual envelopes containing all manner of prayers and well wishes rallied our spirits. Finally, February relinquished to March.

The winds outside still shot brutal gusts of frigid air, and in the north, there were no spring buds on branches. But the calendar promised renewed life. Perhaps I would see the shiny faces of yellow daffodils after all.

March 17, 2014, St. Patrick's Day, fell on a Monday. Julie, her husband Alex, and their children, would spend a four-day weekend with us. Scott had left Minnesota on Saturday, March 15th, and Mark, early on Sunday the 16th, heading for home and back to work. By now, we'd all gotten used to a typical routine as each of our kids brought their families to see us in rotation. But this time would prove different.

It's odd how a single telephone call can completely change the course of your life. Missing an important call can do exactly the same thing — only in an opposite way. In some instances, you experience both, dramatizing the way events turn out even more.

Depending on who you ask, what I'm about to tell you, now humorous in hindsight, was either my fault, Julie's, or her husband Alex's. As much as I love my son-in-law, I prefer to blame him — at least it's a lot more fun to tell the story that way. Frankly, none of us really knows how things happened — the magnitude of our emotions affected our memories.

But regardless of whose fault it was, because of what happened, it could have cost me my life. Let's just say while it took place, I wasn't always so Minnesota nice.

I'm simply glad God maintains control when I do not, maybe that's why He tells me to sit still and wait on Him. Thankfully, He doesn't wait for me to stop talking before He acts on my behalf.

ISAIAH 65:24 (HCSB)
"Even before they call, I will answer;
while they are still speaking, I will hear."

CHAPTER SEVENTEEN

The Silent Ringer

Most people go to one of two extremes with death. They either avoid all thoughts and conversation about it, hoping it will go away if they ignore it. Or they obsess over the subject. As a family we've been forced to learn a healthier balance in our perceptions of dying, death, and the afterlife.

We now know it's as important to talk about how a crisis impacts us emotionally, as it is to discuss the event itself. We have to face our pain in order to heal. But it's equally important to make sure we can handle it — timing is critical to thriving in spite of coming out of a traumatizing situation.

For the Perkins' family, humor is one of the ways we deal with our emotions in a healthy way. It took time before we were ready, but now we can laugh at some of the parts of the story I'm about to share.

As I said, our daughter, Julie, her husband, Alex, and our grandchildren, Aiden, Claire, and sixteen-month-old Madelyn, were visiting over a four-day weekend. Our sons, Mark and Scott, were back home in Missouri holding down our family banking business and spending much needed time with their families.

By Sunday, Julie, much like me, was feeling restless. The date was March 16, 2014, and I wanted to go to the Mall of America with my family. I was tired of focusing on my disease, and I wanted a day to just be a husband, dad, and grandfather.

I was also tired of the main conversation piece being the tone of my skin. Even now, I hate it when someone approaches me and says, "Are you okay, you look pale." Or, "You must be feeling better, your color looks great."

Sick or healthy, I want to be treated like a man, not a diseased person. If you want to help someone, don't treat them like an invalid. I think it's more respectful to show someone dignity, instead of making him feel devalued because he's ill.

That day, I wanted to have a simple meal and act a little silly. For a few hours, I needed to feel normal.

Julie wanted to go to the mall, too. Alex is from Kentucky; so, he wanted to watch the University of Kentucky play Florida for the championship in the SEC men's basketball tournament.

We went to the mall. Julie took Madelyn to look around, while Linda shopped with Claire. But Alex had no interest in meandering, he immediately hunted down a place to watch the game. He spotted a Hooter's restaurant, grabbed Aiden's hand and told me, "The game doesn't start for another hour. I'll take Aiden to a couple of stores; then, we'll go to the restaurant to watch the game and have a snack. If you want to join us, come on up."

I didn't feel up to a lot of walking, so I meandered toward the restaurant while my son-in-law scurried off with my grandson, heading to various mall shops. I didn't know if I had the strength to make it to Hooter's. But finally, I got there.

I peered in the window. Alex and Aiden were already seated. I shuffled to join them.

Alex had a concerned look on his face as I approached. He

said, "You look beat, like you're hating life right now."

"I shouldn't be doing this. My legs hurt. I'm so tired," I told him.

"Well, sit down, rest, relax, and watch the game with us. Let's have a snack."

The waitress came to take our orders — wings and drinks. But before she left to fill them, I asked her if I could take a picture with her to send to my friend, Kem. Joking around with him usually perks me up.

I asked Alex to take a couple of pictures with my phone to send to Kem. He accepted my cell when I offered it, snapped the shots, and tried to send one. But he couldn't get it to go through. We both tried. I'm sure we looked like a couple of country bumpkins arguing over why it wouldn't work.

Julie walked in with Madelyn, while we were trying to send the photo, and eventually was able to take my phone, get the shot moved to her cell, and text Kem directly. What none of us knew, was somewhere in the chaos of passing the phone around three sets of hands, unknown to any of us, we messed something up. The ringer was shut off.

Remember me telling you how a call, or a missed one, could change your life? The silencing of my ringer would become a critical piece of my transplant equation.

Linda and Claire came to the restaurant just as we were finishing our photo texting escapade, so our whole group was now together again. Most of us wanted to go home. But our granddaughter, Claire, wanted to go to the indoor amusement park for one more ride before we left. So we split up.

Julie and Alex took the grandkids for a final spin around the mall, while Linda and I went to use the restroom. It takes about an hour and a half to drive from Minneapolis to Rochester, and we were already exhausted. We just wanted to get back to the condo, no pit stops.

We found out later that Alex took Claire for a last ride

while Julie waited by perusing more of the mall with Aiden in hand, pushing Madelyn in a stroller. Julie was on the escalator when her cell rang. She looked at the number, but she didn't recognize it.

She spoke out loud to herself, "Who's calling from Minnesota?"

It didn't occur to her that it might be connected to my organs.

I'd been on the transplant list for several weeks, and the initial anticipation had worn off. Given enough time, it's strange how much pain and anxiety can become a new normal, even to the point you stop recognizing their sensations.

So in the relaxed environment of a day at the mall, at a point where illness and waiting had become a routine part of our existence, my daughter's mind was no longer in urgent mode. Besides, her number wasn't documented with Mayo.

When the paperwork was filed with the hospital, Mayo had taken our sons, Mark and Scott's phone numbers. But not Julie's, because she wasn't there — it was her turn to stay home in Missouri. So after the clinic couldn't reach me due to my silenced ringer, the hospital called Scott, though he was now the one home in Missouri.

Scott gave the hospital Julie's cell number. Then he got to work making flight and car rental arrangements, so he and Mark could drive to Minnesota immediately. I can only imagine how tough this must have been on my sons. Of course I knew none of that while I was at the mall trying to enjoy our day out.

Julie's phone rang insistently. Still perplexed as to who from Minnesota might be calling, she answered hesitantly, "Hello?"

The voice on the other end got straight to the point. "Are you with your mom and dad?"

"Sort of. We're at the Mall of America. But we're separated right now. I can find them though."

"I'm with the transplant team at Mayo, and I think we have a heart for your dad."

My grown daughter squealed out loud in the mall, "You what?"

"But you have to be here by 7:00 p.m., not a minute later."

Julie looked at her watch, it was just after 5:00 p.m. She knew the drive to Rochester would take an hour and a half under normal driving conditions. Plus, we were all separated in the largest mall in the United States. There was not a second to waste.

Julie tugged on Aiden's arm and bounced sixteen-month-old Maddi's stroller into a high speed jolt. "Come on. We've gotta go. Hurry. Let's go." Dragging my poor grandson behind her, she took off running. While she dialed one-handed while pushing Maddi's stroller, Julie first tried her mom, then me. Unable to reach either one of us, she called her husband.

Just as Alex and Claire got in line for the ride, his phone rang, and he saw it was Julie.

"Hey," he answered casually.

But Alex immediately went into high alert as he tried to understand Julie's fast, breathless, jumbles.

She shouted, "Oh. Oh, my gosh. Dad. Dad got a heart. You need to get to the car. Right now."

Alex had the car keys in his pocket. So he scooped Claire off of the ground then shouted, "Excuse me. Excuse us," as he brushed past people to get out of the ride line. Our son-in-law sprinted through the Mall of America, with his daughter jostling in his arms.

Julie reached Linda and me first. We were standing at the exit, inside the double door foyer, leading to the parking garage. As Julie approached, releasing the grip she had on Aiden's hand and Maddi's stroller, Linda and I were both pointing at our phones, then at each other, while we chattered back and forth. We were trying to figure out why our phones weren't working properly. We'd only discovered this fact seconds before.

By the time Julie got to us, her own telephone was nearly dead. But she had just enough juice to make one more very important call.

Hands shaking, she hit send. "I just found Mom and Dad, we're on the way. We're running to the car now." The phone died at that moment. There wasn't enough power for Julie to hear the Mayo nurse's response.

Breathing hard from running so long, Alex skittered to a stop and put Claire on the floor as they gathered with us in the mall foyer. For about three seconds, everyone stood motionless, except to look at each other in turn. I think we were all in shock.

Then I reacted as I do when I'm flustered and nervous. I often pop off with a sarcastic comment, meant to be funny, although sometimes I miss the mark — especially when I target a specific person. This time, Alex received the brunt of my tongue.

"Alex, you turned my phone off. I can't believe this. If I don't get this heart, I'm going to haunt you for the rest of your life."

My son-in-law was smart enough to know there was no time for a retort to my morbid humor. Alex stepped up. "You guys wait right here, I'll get the car."

It felt as if everything was orchestrated. Julie and Alex were meant to be with us that weekend. Even though things happened dramatically with no extra time, and there were many scary moments, things still came together in the end.

I think there's a life lesson in that. God sometimes provides in crazy ways, so we can't possibly mistake His hand in it. Of course the craziness was far from done — we still had to try and make it to Rochester by 7:00 p.m. — not one minute later. And time was getting away from us.

The next scenes played out like something in a movie. Alex

sprinted out of the mall toward the parking garage. He must have run fast, because what seemed like only a couple of minutes later, he pulled up to the door.

We rushed the car, swarmed the vehicle, opened the three passenger doors simultaneously, and hopped in. To an outsider, we probably looked like New Yorkers fighting for a cab on a busy Manhattan street corner, or a band of sloppy bank robbers trying to make our getaway.

Seat buckles were still clicking as Alex hit the gas, all four tires squealed when we sped away, though he carefully watched for pedestrians and other cars. Alex shot toward the highway — he was carrying us to hope.

A heart was waiting for me at Mayo. The question was, *Would we make it in time?*

JOHN 5:6 (NKJV)
When Jesus saw him lying there, and knew that he already had been in that condition a long time, He said to him, "Do you want to be made well?"

CHAPTER EIGHTEEN

Highway to Hope

The drive itself was an adventure. While Alex swerved in and out of traffic, voices were shouting over each other inside the car.

"Go fast, Daddy," one of the kids yelled.

An adult corrected, "But don't go too fast. It won't matter, if we don't arrive alive."

"Don't get pulled over, we don't have time to explain this to a cop."

"We might have to put the flashers on and outrun them."

Aiden piped up over everyone else, "You can do it, Dad. Go. Go!"

As I listened to my family's voices, I sensed the overwhelmingness of the moment. I didn't realize I spoke my next thought aloud. "I feel so much pressure that this has to go right."

My daughter leaned forward and patted my shoulder. In a gentle voice, she said, "It's going to be okay, Dad. We're all scared to death. We're getting ready to walk into the unknown, and there's no turning back. But we're in it together."

Then a brilliant thought occurred to someone. To this day, none of us are sure whose idea it was.

"Should we call Jerry Beers and have him pray with us?"

"That's a great plan."

He answered by the second ring. "Jerry speaking."

Julie spoke for us. "Dad got a heart. We're on our way to the hospital."

"That's great."

"It's going to be close. We just left Minneapolis, and we have to be in Rochester no later than 7:00 p.m. Could you say a prayer for us?"

"Of course."

Father,

We thank you for providing a heart for Paul, while we pray for the donor's family, who is right now experiencing a deep loss. Please comfort them in this, their hour of need. Let them feel your arms wrap around them in supernatural peace, and let many people offer them solace in their grief.

We also ask you to help Paul arrive at the hospital in plenty of time, while giving he and his family safe travels. We praise you for causing his body to accept this new organ as it is transplanted. Guide the hands and minds of the medical teams who are preparing to do this life-saving work. Thank you for their commitment and sacrifice. We are humbled by your mercies, and ask that your will be done, in Jesus' name.

Amen.

Though he appeared composed at the time, Alex later confessed how powerful his emotions were that night, as they welled up inside of him. He said his heart was thumping, and his eyes were beginning to tear up enough to distort his vision. He had to swipe to clear them. Then he thought to himself, *I can't get emotional — not right now. I have to focus. I have to get them there. I have a job to do, everyone's counting on me.*

I don't think anyone had a clue, as we were all experiencing similar feelings. We were on a highway to hope — the unknown is a scary place to venture.

And then Jerry's voice, clear, strong, and sure in faith cut through the apprehension and settled our nerves. God cleared our minds, and He cleared the way to Mayo.

With concentrated effort, and Jerry's prayer guiding him through, Alex got us to the door at approximately 6:20 p.m. I think he worked our guardian angels overtime, as he shaved nearly twenty minutes off of our drive. The moment Alex brought the car to a stop, Linda, Julie, and I spilled out.

The kids were yelling, "Bye, PaPa. Bye. We love you."

Then Alex, who later said he was suddenly struck by the thought, *I may never see him again. I need to give him a hug or something,* got out and grabbed me. I think we were both shocked as we clenched shoulders.

My son-in-law mumbled, "I love ya."

He said later of that event, "I'll never forget that moment of knowing how precious life is, and how much we should treasure family. Paul doesn't treat me like someone who married into his family, he treats me like a member of it."

Alex is right — he didn't marry into our family, he is family. In any difficult situation, if your eyes are open to seeing it, there is at least one benefit that can result, I believe it's part of God's bigger plan.

One of the positives that came from my illness, was confirmation of Alex's place in our family unit. It even impacted his relationship with my wife, Linda. He saw some of her attributes that I fell in love with.

He said of her, "Linda teaches you how to love people in a different way. She's not touchy, feely, and lovey-dovey, like my mom. But she is the most generous woman I've ever met. Not just with money, but with her time and energy."

Just before we were leaving for Minnesota, a few weeks before the heart transplant, Alex hugged Linda and said, "I love you."

"I love you too," she said.

It was the first time those words were ever exchanged between them both. It's possible those feelings wouldn't have been expressed between them if I hadn't gotten sick. Just as I doubt he would have hugged me and said he loved me outside Mayo, if not for the dramatic events on March 16, 2014.

Don't tell him I told you, but even though I like to razz him, I really do love that boy. I still say he's the one who turned my cell phone ringer off. But I guess I have to forgive him, since he delivered me to my transplant in time.

I learned and re-learned many lessons through my transplant and death journeys. Periods of laughter are important, no matter what you're going through. If the unwell person is open to it, giving them mental breaks through laughter can take their minds off of their problems for just a little while.

It's also helpful to remember that when someone is ill, sometimes they want to be treated like a regular human being, instead of a sick person. It rejuvenates them. It gives them strength to push through the next hard moment when it arrives.

The highway of hope is littered with many turns and unexpected twists, hills and valleys, sections of seriousness and roads to laughter. No matter what region we're in, we all need someone to share the ride. I finally had to admit that to myself and to others.

I knew this by the time we arrived outside the doors of Mayo when the big call came. My new heart was waiting, and as I would soon find out, so was a kidney. But new organs didn't mean instant healing. Another desperate hour was coming.

I had never told my family about what happened to me during my first death so many years before. We hurried into the hospital and found out where we were supposed to go. We stepped on the elevator, and someone pushed the right button. As we rose, so did my emotions. I was excited, but anxiety accompanied it. In hindsight, it's almost like my soul knew what was coming next.

ROMANS 8:28 (NKJV)
"And we know that all things work together
for good to those who love God, to those who
are the called according to His purpose."

CHAPTER NINETEEN

Surviving a Double Transplant

When you're on an organ transplant list, and the call comes, things move quickly. Though you've imagined what it might feel like as you endured all manner of physical and psychological tests, and you've fought impatience for weeks, months, or even years, when it actually happens, reality blindsides you.

All of my actions took place inside an emotional bubble. Some of the pre-surgery details are a bit foggy for me. I think I was in shock.

I remember stepping off the elevator. As we approached the desk, we were directed to an area so we could complete last minute paperwork. I was admitted; then, a swarm of medical people streamed in and out of my room.

They scoured, disinfected, put the IV in my arm, marked my body for surgery, and dressed me in a hospital gown, before they pushed my gurney down the hall in the wee hours of the morning, meds dripping into my veins. The date was now, Monday, March 17, 2014 — St. Patrick's Day.

Legend says the tradition of "the wearing of the green" on

St. Patrick's Day originated from the man for whom the holiday bears his name. He was a fifth century Christian missionary and bishop who used the three leaf shamrock to explain the Holy Trinity to pagan Ireland. He was passionate that they know all three aspects of God's character, as Father, Son, and the Holy Spirit.

Patrick "found God" while enslaved, but he escaped and made his way home to Roman Britain, the area of Great Britain ruled by the Roman Empire at the time. Patrick eventually returned to Ireland, where he used the symbol of the shamrock to represent the fullness of God's love, grace, and power. He became a mighty warrior for God.

Considering Patrick's story, it's fitting that my surgeries took place on this date. I, too, was enslaved. Not by other people, but by misaligned priorities. I knew Jesus, but I still hadn't overcome my fears and insecurities enough to tell others what He had done for me, as Patrick did. But that was getting ready to change.

What had seemed an eternity of waiting, now felt like warp speed as I was whisked into the operating room. My nephrologist was in the middle of another surgery, so I was scheduled to receive my kidney after my new heart. Originally the procedures were supposed to take place the other way around.

Years, months, weeks, and days now dwindled down to hours. Mark and Scott didn't get to see me before I was whisked into surgery, but I understand they made it right before my double transplant got underway.

The anesthesia did its work — until I died during surgery. Again.

It was then I saw the multi-colored lights before floating out of body above the hospital gurney.

I heard a doctor say, "He's not going to make it," before directing the surgical nurses to disconnect me when they were ready.

I could see my new heart inserted into my chest cavity — refusing to pump in and out.

The doctors left the room, shoulders sagging low, sadness hushing their whispers.

Two nurses went about the business of unhooking me, reverently attending my body, even while they discussed everyday gossip. It miffed me that they ignored me while I insisted I wasn't gone.

Ultimately, I experienced my own funeral.

I don't know exactly how I returned to life in the physical realm. I never saw how my new heart started its bumps against my chest. I didn't view the first intake of breath after the rise and fall of my lungs began again. I didn't feel blood recharge its burrow through my veins. I entirely missed the placement of my new kidney as it was transplanted after my heart.

To this day, I don't know precisely how long I was dead, I just know a lot happened while I was gone. And as suddenly as I was transported outside of my physical body, it seemed I was equally thrust back inside. For me, mere moments passed before consciousness caused my eyes to flutter open in a too-bright hospital room.

I didn't know it, but while I was observing my own death, then enjoying a euphoric release from my body, my family was enduring hell in the hospital.

They had expected a long wait, since a heart transplant is no easy task. But not knowing exactly what was going on made the hours seem to tick even slower. More than once, someone wondered out loud, "You'd think they'd at least give us an update."

Finally, once all danger had passed, a man in a white coat went to the waiting room and told my wife and kids that I almost didn't make it into the second surgery. With great compassion, he said, "We lost your husband during the transplant. But thankfully, we were able to revive him. He's alive. For now.

We're not sure how things will turn from here — but for the time being, he's stabilized."

My wife and children had been awake for over twenty-four hours when they were finally allowed to see me. I was out of it, and I would be for a while.

After much healing, Linda told me of that first entry into my room, "When we entered the room, we thought you looked good, compared to your previous post-op conditions. At this point, we had no idea just how much you'd gone through."

Julie posted a gratitude prayer on Facebook, March 18, 2014, the day after my transplant.

Dear God, Thank you for the many blessings you have given our family, especially the gift of life for my dad. What an amazing, but emotional journey our family has been on over the last three years. He still has lots of healing yet to do, so please continue to be with him during this time of need. This has been a hard couple of days, knowing that a life was taken in order to save my dad. But the donor family not only gave a gift of life to my dad, they gave a gift of life to many others. We are forever thankful for them. My dad's chest was finally closed this afternoon. He recognized our voices this morning, and even opened his eyes and moved his head. We are hoping that he will be awake tomorrow.

I wouldn't wake up the next day. Not fully.

It's amazing what we take for granted: the ability to nod our head, blink our eyes, move our toes, understand and respond to verbal commands. All of these things were big achievements for me as I lay in my hospital bed. Another huge feat took place when I heard the voice of a little child.

A week after my transplant, our oldest son, Mark, brought his boys up for spring break. They drove from Missouri to Minnesota to see me. But at the time, I wasn't receptive.

Mark and my grandsons arrived in Rochester on that

Monday night. Mark took one boy at a time to see me — their Papa — while the other stayed with Linda.

Johnny, the youngest, went in first. They said when I heard Johnny's voice, I opened my eyes. Then I reached out for his hand. At first my six-year-old grand-boy was scared. But Mark assured him, "It's okay. He just wants to hold your hand."

So the little boy slipped his tiny fingers into my large, but fragile paw. Johnny lit up.

Then I dozed off again, and my hand relaxed off of Johnny's hand. So Johnny walked to the other side of the bed and picked up my other hand. I opened my eyes again.

As he held my hand, Johnny's head began to bob up and down, while he scoured the area above my bed.

Mark asked, "What are you doing, son?"

"Counting the tubes." Johnny noted the spider web of black, white, and clear connectors linked to various body parts from my head to my feet.

When he finished bobbing, Johnny looked at the nurse and said, "There's forty-two tubes in my Papa."

The nurse smiled and said, "There's going to be forty-one tomorrow if I have my way."

After that, my family monitored my progress by how many tubes were still left in my body. It all started with Johnny.

James entered next. Intrigued with all of the equipment, noises, and movements of the hospital staff, he stared in awe, barely able to say a word. I hope he knows how much his presence meant to his Papa.

I'm glad Mark's boys came then, because I had a huge setback that night. The medical staff took out my breathing tube, and I began to run a high fever. By early Tuesday morning, I had such a tough time, they had to put the breathing tube back in, and put me into a medically induced coma. Once again, my family didn't know whether I would make it. Linda's journal filled in more gaps.

A few days later, after the kids once again returned home to tend to their own lives, the doctors at Mayo took out your ventilator and gave you a tracheotomy. You didn't tolerate it well, and neither did I.

It was hard to watch my husband fight for breath. I kept wondering why they didn't get me out of there, and it was a real low point. Especially when they ended up putting the ventilator back in. It was then I fled the room. I had to get out of there, I couldn't take anymore.

Once I'd spent some time alone praying and thinking, I was able to gather the strength to go back in. After we made it through that day, I was able to stay by your side. It helped that I wasn't alone too many days, as our three children, plus some close friends and other family members, took turns coming and going.

When I finally showed improvement, Linda updated everyone on Facebook.

Paul is waking up and becoming more alert. They finally removed the breathing tube from his throat around noon on Saturday. He had become attached to it, so he got anxious when they removed it.

They tried sitting him in a chair, but that only lasted fifteen minutes. They also used a bigger tube to increase the flow of oxygen through his nose than we are used to seeing. He had to practice breathing deeper and slower, but he's getting better at it now.

They are also still pulling fluids off through dialysis, helping his body transition to using the new kidney.

Yesterday, he kept mouthing, "I love you." Then his lips formed the words, "Am I going to make it?"

He didn't get much sleep last night. He was afraid he wouldn't wake up. Besides having a touch of pneumonia, anxiety and depression are normal parts of the recovery process after a major surgery.

Today, he was awake much of the morning, and was able to talk just above a whisper. I already had to get on to him though. Paul kept smiling at the nurses, so I warned them that he can be quite flirty.

He sat up on the side of the bed, and asked for something to drink and ice chips, he also mentioned eating food. But they wouldn't let him have anything yet.

After he was settled back in bed, he asked, "How am I doing?"

When the nurse responded, "You're doing well," Paul seemed satisfied.

He spent most of the evening sleeping peacefully. We praise God for these small steps to independence. Thank you for your thoughts and prayers.

As I started to show progress, the push from my family began. When my will faltered, theirs kicked in.

In the hospital, when I would say, "I'm done. I'm tired of this. I'm ready to go home and die," they called me out by turning my own strategies on me.

My boys and my brother, John, conspired by setting tiny goals that felt like mountain-climbing to me.

"If you eat your oatmeal today, you'll get eggs and bacon soon."

Mark remembered when I had come out of my after-death experience in St. Louis, and he said. "I want to go camping and wake up the next morning to the smell of bacon."

John told me, "If you drink your water and can pee, they'll take the catheter out."

Scott encouraged, "If you get out of bed and walk a few steps, they'll mark your chart with an "atta boy." Everything you do gets you one step closer to them releasing you and you getting out of here healthy."

It did make me happy to achieve each little goal. I felt inspired as the satisfaction of accomplishing something each day strengthened me mentally. Of course, I wasn't going to tell them at that time.

Mark later confessed that he and his Uncle John had schemed. He said, "We ultimately gave him a release date as a goal to work toward. This was not something we discussed with the doctors, just a plan hatched by two men desperate to save a third. And it worked.

The goals were not written down, but a mental map with dates was discussed on a regular basis between us. It prodded him to move above his circumstances."

During this period, I often felt helpless and out of control. I'm used to being big and strong, not helpless as an infant. I admit I was cranky — and worse. Being an invalid was my worst fear. Plus, I wasn't getting much sleep. My body was worn down. I was consumed with the unknown. Many times, I felt as if I were losing it. But then my family would step in to save me from the torture of my own mind.

Unbeknownst to anyone else, one of my inner struggles was what I was missing. During my transplant surgery and my second after-life experience, I was allowed another brief visit to a place of euphoria, where there is no more sorrow, no more pain, and no more tears. (Revelation 21:4)

It didn't help that when I was returned to this planet so I could serve God and my fellow man, things didn't start off easy. Like any incredible outcome, adversity was required first — some of it I wasn't sure I would survive or if I wanted to.

March 17, 2014, the date of my double transplant, started me on the path to a new life. But my trials were far from over. More physical, emotional, and spiritual hurdles were coming — but then again, so were more amazing miracles. Greater than anything I could have imagined.

REVELATION 21:4 (NIV)
"He will wipe every tear from their eyes.
There will be no more death or mourning or crying or pain,
for the old order of things has passed away."

CHAPTER TWENTY

Training or Torture

One of the most challenging things for the hospital staff at this point was to adjust my medications correctly. The most challenging for me — eating.

My transplants were fourteen days earlier. Still, I hadn't ingested anything since Julie told us about the phone call at the mall.

In my croaking tone, I pleaded with the nurses. "I'm starving, can't I at least have a popsicle? I'd give anything for one."

"Sorry, Mr. Perkins. You can't have anything by mouth until after your swallow study. We must determine it's safe for you."

One of the nurses ran a chilled sponge over my parched lips. It felt good, but I was desperate for real liquid.

By my estimation, things seemed grim at this stage of my recovery. I didn't feel like I was getting better fast enough. I remember thinking, *These surgeries were supposed to make me feel better. After what I went through in 2011, I thought this would be easier. But I'm not sure it is.*

Sickness affects me oddly. When I feel bad, it seems like

I've never felt worse in my life. When I feel good, I can't recall just how awful I felt when I crossed into a state of chronic discomfort.

Briefly after my transplants, I thought I would never recover — and I believed it would be pointless to exert more effort.

Two weeks post-surgery, my wife's spirits seemed low. She never complained while she walked through it. But later, I discovered she was frustrated. However, as hard as it was on both of us, there were rare moments of humor.

She said it was hard to keep a straight face when she was in my room after hearing some of the things I said to the nurses. She didn't know if I was serious or joking, and she didn't dare ask.

I don't remember what I said, much less why I said any of it.

Linda's journal entry March 31, said, "Guess we will start off this third week with positives. We aren't there yet, but we do appreciate the thoughts, cards, and prayers from all of you."

The petitions and kind words helped, because two days later, on April 2, I sat up. Then I stood briefly with help.

They removed my trach on April 10. And on April 11, 2014, I was finally moved from ICU to a step-down room at Mayo. I also navigated from the bed to a chair in a standing position, pivoted, and walked with assistance. It was a big day.

My heart was working well, and my new kidney was catching up. I only required dialysis every two to three days. Slowly, but determinedly, I worked with my therapists toward one goal — going home. I hoped things would get easier once I went home, but I still had miles ahead of me. A miracle first requires a problem, and I would encounter more of each before my strength returned.

On April 27, 2014, the Mayo Clinic released me to my family's care. But we had to stay in our Rochester apartment for at least three months. It's crucial for a transplant patient to keep all post-surgery appointments and follow up with measurement tests.

I knew from Dr. Borgeson's pre-surgery review how fortunate I was to have a strong social support system. It can mean the difference between life and death — between a good quality of life and feeling depressed to the point of wanting to die. But when I arrived home my family was almost too strong.

My wife's words below indicate that I was not an easy person to manage when I was released from the hospital.

***

"When Paul recovered enough for us to return to our small apartment in Rochester, it didn't take long for me to figure out I needed to screen and intervene his interactions with others. Thank goodness our faithful dog, Yadi, kept him occupied much of the time.

Paul's mind and body were relearning how to act properly. While he worked through his recovery, it was obvious he wasn't thinking clearly, believing he should invite people over, entertain, and cook meals for them. I had a problem with that — a big one, for good reason.

He couldn't open a can of soup on his own. He insisted on cooking, except there was no telling what ingredients he might put in his dishes. And he would go on shopping excursions, buying outrageous items or returning with things we already had. I never knew what he might walk in the door carrying. He was especially prone to purchase food he shouldn't eat.

Salty chips were his favorite. Once, while my sisters, Donna and Lisa, along with my niece, Tracie, came to visit so I could escape from my caregiving duties for a few days, they hid his chips. Boy, did he get upset. You would think three female heads and six hands could restrain him, but things got pretty scary. The situation escalated to the point that I had to arrange a flight within eight hours, arriving home a day earlier than planned.

All three unsuspecting females found out the hard way that a six foot four inch recovering transplant patient requires twenty-four hour care. And his salty chips.

The things Paul and I went through behind closed doors, when it was just the two of us, were the toughest. I saw and heard things no one else did. Sometimes, I thought he acted like a petulant child, and he often accused me of not reacting well to his mood swings. We were both in pure survival mode, and that doesn't always look pretty.

I'd threaten to tell doctors, our children, or close friends when he rebelled and didn't do the things he was supposed to. He threatened to call our son, Scott, to come and get me, because I wasn't letting him have his way.

There are many moments I'm glad no one else could see or hear. There were many days when we weren't at our best. Either of us.

As part of the transplant process, Paul went through intense mental screening along with the physical tests, they don't give new hearts to just anyone. Sometimes I think they should have screened me the same way. I'm not sure I was qualified for the task of Paul's caregiver. Thankfully, our kids and friends stepped in and did a lot.

One of the biggest weights I carried was being Paul's watch dog. Transplant teams work hard to ensure recipients treat their new organ like the precious gift it is. So though he took it seriously, and for the most part was extremely cautious, when Paul slacked in the slightest bit, I felt compelled to straighten him out. A part of me wondered if I should keep my mouth shut and let things go. But I felt a huge responsibility, and it tore me up inside.

I'm sure if anyone would have heard us they'd think we sounded silly. We were both stressed-out, physically and emotionally spent.

For a good month, while Paul's body healed, we dealt with his goofiness. We could never predict what he might say or do. My intelligent, strong husband, for a short time, wasn't himself. Sometimes he made me laugh. But sometimes, off to myself, I cried where no one else could see. Thank goodness, we had Yadi to diffuse some of our tenser moments."

***

I wish I had a do-over in the way I treated my wife during my recuperation. The Bible is right — a husband and wife become one. (Ephesians 5:31)

My pain was shared equally by my wife, in a different way, but as severely. I'm deeply sorry for ignoring her needs. I should have protected her more. She deserved better. The rest of my family, however, deserves appreciation, too.

When I was finally healed enough to make the trip back to Missouri, Mark and Scott loaded our truck and Sequoia. Both vehicles were stuffed with clothes, shoes, electronics, medical apparatus, leftover groceries, and gifts from well-wishers. By the time we added our grandchildren, Naomi and Johnny, Linda and myself, each of the boys as a driver, along with my faithful canine companion, Yadi, we may have looked like the Clampett bunch on The Beverly Hillbillies. But I didn't care about appearances, I was still too weak.

Well people can't truly understand your feelings in painful moments. My sons, Scott and Mark, and my brothers, John and Joe, had no idea just how terrible I felt when I came home. But in hindsight, I'm glad they didn't — their push was something I needed.

From the time my children were young, I urged them to do more than they believed they were capable of. I forced them out of their comfort zones. Little did I know, one day, our roles would reverse. I suspect they thought turnabout was fair play during my recovery.

When I came home, I had to rebuild my weakened muscles from months of being confined to a hospital bed. My entire body needed work. I could barely raise a two-pound dumb bell. It was devastating for me to be in such bad shape.

My oldest son, Mark, and his younger brother, Scott, encouraged me when I was ready to give up.

Mark would say, "Dad, here's the deal. You can sit here and watch TV until you die before your time — until your body finally fails you. Or you can work on yourself, fight through this, until you're finally able to pick up a golf club again."

Both of the boys made me go a bit longer when I wanted to quit working out. They would motivate me with, "Just give it ten more minutes. You can go ten more minutes."

As mad as that made me, I complied.

They also used my grandchildren as motivators.

Mark would say, "Do you want to see your grandkids play ball?"

More than once, Scott undermined my pity party. "Do you want to see your grandchildren grow up or not?"

This threat was enough to inspire me. I would repeat out loud, "I'm doing this for my grandkids. I'm only doing this for my grandkids."

I'd make it through one more exercise, and day by day, I became a little stronger — physically and mentally.

In those first days at home, Mark and Scott had to help lift me, because Linda couldn't do it. And I certainly couldn't help myself. I was so weak I didn't even want to lift a spoon to my mouth most of the time.

I had lost my drive during the lengthy hospital stay.

Linda did everything I asked, but the others knew unless I was pushed I would regress. They didn't let me get away with the things my wife succumbed to.

I found out later that Mark would tell Linda to leave and

take a break so he could push me or rebuke me for being mean to her. While it was happening, I didn't realize how disrespectful I was to my wife, but my son clearly let me know.

Linda would call Mark bawling, saying, "Dad did this . . . ., Dad did that . . . ."

Then I'd get on the phone with Mark to defend myself. I'd shout, "Well, she did this . . . ."

But Mark didn't allow himself to get sucked into the drama.

When I whined to defend my poor behavior, Mark would say, "Be the bigger person. Be the man. Relax. Don't forget how rough this is for Mom, too. I know it's hard on you physically, but it's mentally hard on her."

On my toughest days, my three children and other family members reminded me I should fight to live.

More than once I was asked, "Is this the legacy you want to leave the little ones?"

It was not. Yet, I still struggled with some tough questions.

I asked my family repeatedly. "Why did God save me? They gave me less than one percent chance of survival — why was I given a miracle? Why do other people die under better conditions than what I had? What is the purpose for me living?"

My brother, John, along with the rest of my family and friends, helped me wade through my emotions, reminding me that purpose is often revealed through pain. But they weren't always easy on me.

John's military and governmental intelligence background influenced his opinions. However, there's a reason those disciplines work — for civilians as well as those in service.

John puts it this way:

> *We use a temptation or tendency too often as a justification to make a decision to do something unhealthy, for us, or for someone else. We use too many things as crutches, excuses to act in inappropriate ways. When the results aren't what we desire, or there's a negative consequence,*

we get angry, and point outward, instead of looking inward to take responsibility, and prepare ourselves to do something different in the future, so we can experience a better outcome.

Military discipline taught me how to push through difficult conditions. My training helps me take my mindset to a higher level. I believe this is different than the ways psychology teaches.

In the military, for those recruited for risk-taking positions, there is a criteria to perform despite how you feel, this conditioning means there's a much lower incidence of depression and anxiety for those who fill those roles. What I tried to do with my brother, was use the mental skills I learned during my service, to drive Paul.

When you want to motivate someone who is losing their will to live, you must lead them through your own positive example, and resolve to make the most of each day. Leading only happens by example, mere words are meaningless without actions to back them up.

With Paul, when he was depressed, I challenged him to meet specific goals. Paul was resistant to my suggestions at first, but I could tell after I left, my words echoed in Paul's mind, and he pondered the challenges I made.

We didn't see immediate results, as a unified family unit, we had to be patient and look for small signs of progress, but over time, day by day, the results came. It never works to try and numb your pain, or avoid your situation, true healing only comes when you face your pain, and as a family, we needed to respectfully yet determinedly help my brother do that.

There is a difference between those who are ill, and those in peril due to dangerous situations. Sickness comes from within, peril comes without. But regardless of what you are facing, a strong desire to live can help you survive many things.

In Vietnam, men with survivable wounds but with a weaker will to live would die, whereas, those with much graver injuries would survive. Circumstances may arise where we must fight to live — Paul's certainly required it. But Paul's condition also required something else of him.

There's a core strength we can grip when we have faith. Without faith, there's no hope to hold onto. When you know Jesus, and you ask Him to help you, God is either going to pull you through a circumstance, or He's going to deliver you into the Promised Land. Strength is the bedrock of faith, weakness denies it.

I start each day by saying, "Thank you, Lord, for allowing me to wake up again."

It helps me begin with a happy attitude, and maintain a grateful heart.

John inspired me many days when I didn't want to hear his inspiration, but he gave me what I needed, instead of what I wanted. So did my brother, Joe.

Joe called me often, and told me what I should and shouldn't do. It was usually the last thing I wanted to hear. Mostly, his bossing made me angry, until his words had the chance to roll around in my head, making me think about things a little more logically than I was capable of on my own. I recognized the truth when I heard it, even when I didn't want to act on it.

My family and closest friends kept me from giving up. But they didn't only drive me, sometimes they helped me relax.

Laughter helps the healing process. Most of us realize humor is good for the mind, body, and soul, but we don't always know how to engage ourselves. It often takes an outsider to break through our somber moods.

My family and friends used laughter to help me survive tough days, even when I didn't want to laugh. They exercised my emotions with humor, while they trained my body with physical activity. Of course, perspective is everything. What they called training, I sometimes called torture. But I'm glad they didn't give up.

Through the complexity and longevity of my illness, together as a family, we learned how to navigate the scary, quirky, and humorous events. We also grew in gratitude.

During dark days, I wish I could have celebrated the miracle of breath in my body, instead of beating myself up for not having the ability to do more. But in hindsight, I know I did my best. I'm learning patience with others and myself.

One thing embedded in my life now is thankfulness and a heart of prayer. Especially for one group of loving people.

As Linda put it so perfectly, "We especially thank God and pray for my donor's family, as they are part of our miracle too."

ROMANS 12:12
"Rejoice in hope, be patient in tribulation,
be constant in prayer."

CHAPTER TWENTY-ONE

My Hero, Cooper

My greatest hero died too young. I owe my life to a young man named Cooper, or as his family and friends often called him, Coop Man, Coop, or Coops. Taken too soon, who sacrificed for others all his life.

In death, Cooper gave life — and in his life, he offered hope.

Many fear having their organs removed and given to someone else upon their death. However, donating your organs can add purpose and meaning to your life. They become a lasting legacy — for someone in desperate need, and a symbol of courage to your grieving loved ones.

I'm blessed to have learned about Cooper. Not all families are willing to connect with the recipient when their beloved's organs have been transplanted into a stranger's body. This is understandable, and it should be respected. However, in my case, I am honored that Coop's mom, dad, and siblings responded to my communication request through our coordinating agency.

When Cooper's mom answered my letter, I discovered the loving family who lost their twenty-year-old son and brother. His memory is preserved. But because of his family's bravery, he's also alive in me, as well as several other organ and tissue recipients.

Because of the sacrifice Cooper's family made, I must live my life in such a way as to esteem him and respect those left behind to mourn. I will spend every possible moment making the most of the extra time I've been given. I pray many are inspired to do more than they believed possible, because of the gift of life given to me. I can't speak for the other recipients, but I know through my life, Cooper will impact many others.

There are surprises in my new life. Though I haven't changed, I'm not exactly the same person I was before. Cooper's influence is evident.

A moderate eater before, I now have a ravenous appetite. Having always been strategic by nature, I surprise myself with moments of blatant spontaneity. My conservative, minimalist upbringing, refined with the maturity of age, is not so ingrained anymore. Now I am often impulsive like a young man. Why?

Cooper's mom chuckled with the soft laugh of a woman who hadn't expressed joy for a very long time when I described the subtle changes in my behaviors. "My Cooper was impulsive, spontaneous, and he ate constantly. You've definitely got some of him in you."

Cellular memory transference is hotly debated among those in scientific and medical communities. Some contest the idea, based solely on hypothesis, while others vehemently defend the idea of a donor's characteristics transferring to a recipient's body upon transplant. As one who has experienced the phenomenon, I am a believer.

I think many of us fear being changed to the point of extinction from the essence of who we really are. Some would even face death rather than risk losing themselves. But I can speak to those concerns.

You don't lose yourself when you receive traces of your donor's personality, traits, and habits. Instead, they enhance you. And for their loved ones, the gift of these organs provides comfort that a part of them lives on. Your existence becomes a beacon, pointing to a purpose greater than life itself — and to mysteries no one on earth can explain.

You see, Cooper and I have more than his heart and kidney in common. His mom revealed more fascinating facts. For instance, his best friend's name was Paul, like my name. One of the other recipients got Cooper's liver and his other kidney. His name is Paul, too.

My biggest concern was never about carrying someone else's body parts inside of me. I wanted to care for them properly, showing the respect deserving of his family. I wanted to reach out to my donor's family early on, but many questions that plagued me.

How would they feel about me? Would I remind them of their sorrow? Were they beginning to move out of their grief and would I plunge them back into a world smothered in sadness? Would they reject me, because my existence would deepen their mourning?

It was a great relief when I heard from Cooper's mom, "I'm so glad to hear from you."

A hero is someone who willingly sacrifices for the sake of others. My hero's name is Cooper. In my estimation, his family is deserving of that title as well. Cooper's family chose to honor his spirit and pass on his legacy through organ donation. I would not be sharing my story with you today without their compassionate decision.

Cooper's mom, Robin, is valiant in her efforts to encourage others by telling their account of what happened. I hope you are as inspired by the words of a mother who deeply loves and misses her son.

ROMANS 14:8 (NLT)
"If we live, it's to honor the Lord. And if we die, it's to honor the Lord. So whether we live or die, we belong to the Lord."

CHAPTER TWENTY-TWO

In Cooper's Honor

Cooper was our youngest child. I'm Robin, his mom, and his dad's name is Tony. Connor, our oldest son, was followed by twin daughters, Dana, the elder twin by nineteen minutes, born prior to her younger identical sister, Devin. Cooper arrived when Connor was four and the girls were two.

We are an ordinary, hard-working Minnesotan family. Grounded by faith in family and a God we don't always understand, but who we trust through foundational beliefs.

Coop was my fourth and last baby, who arrived wielding the same impact he's making today. It seems he rarely took the easy route, but he always kept life interesting.

At seven pounds four ounces, he wasn't a big baby. But he got the hospital staff's attention nonetheless. He came through the birth canal so fast — Cooper did everything fast — that he sustained minor bruises on his tender infant skin. The discoloration had a blue hue. So once he was placed in the maternity ward bassinet, the nurses pinned a note saying, "Bruised not blue." This was to prevent the shift change crew from panicking, mistakenly believing Cooper was deprived of oxygen. As it was, he was already labeled, "at risk."

An anomaly at the top of Cooper's ears meant the creases above them weren't fully formed. The medical staff placed Cooper in ICU, thinking this pointed to a premature birth. When his pediatrician came in the next day, he said, "I have no idea what they're talking about. This baby is fine."

He was immediately removed from Intensive Care. But that was our Coop, always the center of attention — not because he demanded it — simply by being himself.

Cooper didn't learn to walk like most babies. His first few tottering steps were more of a jog that quickly picked up speed, developing into a full on run. He didn't stop running until his last day.

Early on, Cooper's personality shimmered onto everyone he came in contact with. Coop was magnetizing, he had a way of making people feel like they each had a special bond with him — a sweet boy who grew into a compassionate young man. But who had a mischievous side, too, especially if he could draw a laugh out of someone. The source of Coop Man's greatest pleasure was making life fun for others — he was the king of giving. That's why the decision to donate his tissue and organs wasn't a question for our family.

It just made sense for him to offer the ultimate gift. Many times over.

Cooper's full speed forward way of charging through life kept his body lean, though it sometimes presented challenges. Although temporary setbacks did little to slow him down. When he was two years old, one of his toddler friends was leaving our house to go home. But Cooper wanted him to stay.

Cooper ran to the car after his friend, extending his small hands in a "come to me" gesture, just as the door was closing. Before anyone could stop it, his thumb was caught in the jamb as the door slammed. His favorite sucking thumb.

Needless to say, he was an unhappy little boy for a few minutes as fat tears fell from his sweet, slim cheeks. But he didn't wallow in his pain, refusing to sit still long enough to be nursed. He soon pushed himself off my lap and went back to play. Since Cooper wasn't overly concerned, I took a deep breath and expelled relief — until the next day.

Barney was on TV, and Cooper being Cooper, danced with the big purple dinosaur. Whirling and twirling, Coop sang and giggled in his precious toddler voice, "I love you, you love me, we're a happy family." He began to spin at a run, the scene unfolded before I could move.

I think Cooper may have tripped over his own feet. But whatever the reason, my baby stumbled and fell head first against our brick fireplace. Blood began to gush from his eyebrow area. I scooped him up and saw he needed stitches. So I rushed him to the car, and we headed to the hospital.

After the doctor finished stitching Cooper's cut, I got a glimpse of Cooper's bruised thumb from the door incident the day before. Sheepishly, I lifted his little arm and asked the pediatrician, "Could you look at his thumb while we're here? He caught it in a car door yesterday."

It took about ten seconds for him to say, "Let's get an x-ray."

A few hours later, after films confirmed a break in Cooper's thumb, I walked out of the hospital with my bandage wrapped baby in my arms. His head *and* his thumb. But the fun wasn't over.

My oldest son Connor had a school event that afternoon. I'm sure we were quite the spectacle when I carried Cooper in looking partially like a mummy — but he wasn't phased.

As soon as the Novocaine wore off, my little innovator worked that bandage until he got it off. Our little thumb sucker was once again a happy boy. When he set his mind to something, you weren't going to change it, no matter what. And his overzealous attitude did not end with this stage in his life.

When he was four, away from my watchful eyes, Cooper decided to show some friends how he'd just taught himself to ride a bike. People in the neighborhood reported on what they saw.

Beaming from cheek to cheek, he hopped on his bike and took off. Things were going well, the wind blew through his hair as he flew down the street. It was the sound that alerted people from blocks away that something had gone wrong.

BOOM! Cooper plowed into a construction van down the street. He left a nasty dent in that vehicle, while he walked away unscathed. Thankfully, the owner was as charmed by Cooper as the rest of us, so harsh feelings didn't make things worse. Coop had that effect on people.

As Cooper grew, so did the smiles and waves that followed him.

At an early age, it was easy to see he had a special talent in working with machinery and robotics. He loved all things mechanical. He could recognize any car or truck by its body style, and he loved to hear an engine purr. But Cooper's passions sometimes caused distraction, to the point that homework wasn't always his priority.

Yet, no matter how frustrated his dad and I would get over his grades, we just couldn't stay mad at Cooper very long. However, he kept us on our toes.

When he became a teenager, he begged for a truck. He badgered us constantly. One day he texted, "I need a pick up."

Figuring it was the same tired routine, I texted back sarcastically, "Okay."

A little while later, Cooper walked into the house. He scowled, "Why didn't you get me from school?"

"I didn't know you needed a ride."

"I told you I needed a pick up."

Suddenly my misinterpretation dawned on me. I started laughing, and at first, he wasn't very happy about my humor.

But once Cooper figured out that I thought his text was a repeat of the many other times he'd asked us to get him a truck, he laughed, too. I think he liked my version better.

Eventually, Cooper got his truck. His first one was a green 1996 GMC Sonoma. His vehicles were his greatest treasures on earth. My boy loved his toys — and other people's.

His favorite was his Uncle Mark's 2005 slick black, Chevy SS truck with Cooper 285x50x20 rims. I've never seen a vehicle decked with so many fancy tail lights, emblems, grills, and other shiny accessories. We called it Black Beauty in our family. When Cooper's Uncle Mark passed away, Tony and I bought it. Mark had always said if anything ever happened to him, he wanted Cooper to have it. Though we never officially gave it to Cooper, he had access to it on a regular basis. Black Beauty is still in our family today. And after losing both Mark and Cooper, we have no plans to sell.

Cooper borrowed the Black Beauty often, using any excuse he could muster. Just before Christmas 2012, he came up with yet another reason he needed to use her. We didn't know it, but this time, he did it for us instead of for him.

On Christmas morning, Cooper lead us out to the garage where we kept Black Beauty. He pulled the license plate down to reveal a hidden hitch. It was the perfect gift. Now we could pull our trailer when we went to our favorite camping spot at Cross Lake. Some of our best and last memories as a complete family with Cooper originated around the fire and picnic table there.

It was pictures of Cross Lake that served as a back drop on Cooper's funeral cards, hand-crafted by John, our daughter Dana's boyfriend. They were more fitting than the generic offering from the funeral home. They allowed us to add our own sayings and personal Bible verses, along with Coop's picture on the front. I think he would have liked them.

He also would have liked the way Black Beauty was used

to celebrate his life. Uncle Mike, a fun camping companion, created lettering we placed on the glossy black door of the SS. It simply said, "Coops," just like his Sonoma and toolbox. The truck really stood out parked against the curb. With his affinity for vehicles and all things mechanical, it was an appropriate tribute.

After his funeral service, Cooper's friends wanted to do a Burn Out dedicated to him, like they used to. I guess it was another one of those fun things he did with the guys, but didn't tell Mom. Good thing he worked at a tire place, I suspect he used his discount a time or two. I can actually laugh about it now.

When Cooper was alive, besides mechanical work with his hands, he also required emotional stimulation — he wasn't afraid of his feelings or of getting close to people. Once, when my husband and I went out of town, I came home to a grinning Cooper, who proudly said, "You've got to go look at your screensaver."

Immediately wary, I said, "What did you do?"

"Just look."

I cautiously approached my computer and moved the mouse. My new screensaver popped up. It was a split screen. On one side it had a photo of Cooper's green GMC truck completely torn apart with the caption, "I was lonely and bored. Please don't leave me alone again."

The other side had a picture of his green Sonoma, pristinely put back together. Above the photo it read, "It's okay, but I'm glad you're back home."

He could melt my heart with guilt one second and mend it with his warmth the next. Apparently, I wasn't the only one drawn to his charismatic ways.

After his death, many of his former classmates reported about Cooper's kindness. Whether they were labeled as geeks or jocks, scholars or special needs, it seemed everyone loved

Cooper. Why?

My son took the time to acknowledge people, and to in-clude and protect them. In Cooper's world, bullying wasn't okay, and he refused to tolerate it. You just had a good time when you were in his presence. He tried to make people feel better, and he accepted them as they were, even when they got his name wrong.

Oddly enough, people who didn't know Coop's big broth-er, often called Cooper, Connor. But Coop took it in stride. When asked why he didn't correct people, he shrugged and said, "I knew they were talking to me, and I like Connor, so it's no big deal."

No big deal — that was the essence of Cooper's spirit, keep-ing life light and peaceful. It seemed his greatest purpose was to make others smile, laugh, and have fun.

Cooper was also a dare devil. He was competitive. Athletic, though he didn't play in the sports programs at school. He didn't run track, but he was so fast he once caught a bunny rabbit trying to escape his grasp. He wasn't a hurdler. But un-afraid of heights, he hurled his body from a two-story build-ing, injuring his ankle on impact. I didn't find out about this one until one of his friends confessed at the funeral wake for our son. Cooper's version was that he tripped on a street curb.

I'm sure he and his friends did a few things I don't know about, but I'm grateful to have experienced these wonderful kids.

Paul, Dan, Alex, and Cooper spent a lot of time as a group. Together they made up the fearsome foursome and filled our home with tremendous amounts of laughter. Dianna, his for-mer girlfriend who was and will always be a part of Cooper's life, added to our joy. Even after they broke up, they remained close friends. Plus, from my perspective anyway, the breakup wasn't legal. They talked, texted, and hung out, even after they made it Facebook official.

Our continued relationships with these kids provides on-going comfort. Spurring happy memories of the life force that was Cooper. Our son's spirit was contagious and legendary, so was his appetite. Food was very important to Coop.

His absolute favorite was Cowboy Burgers with bacon, guacamole, pico de gallo, chipotle, mayonnaise, and an on-ion ring. At Thanksgiving, he consumed multiple helpings of green bean casserole. But chicken nuggets, pizza, french fries, and hamburgers also made the list of his faves. He ate mounds of ranch dressing with all of it.

While Cooper was alive, gallons of milk and sixteen ounce bottles of ranch dressing poured like water from a sieve. Our reduced grocery bill is one more way we feel our son's loss. I'd beg, borrow, and steal to stock up on milk and ranch dressing if I could bring Coops here to consume them again.

Cooper was a talker, fast and excitable. He could also be witty and clever. In February, the month before he died, Cooper saw a dentist. While looking back and forth between his x-rays and chart, the dentist said, "Are you sure you had your wisdom teeth pulled?"

Cooper said, "Yeah. All four when I was seventeen. Why?"

The dentist scratched his head, "Well then, you've got two more."

Without missing a beat, Coop shot back, "I guess I have two extras because I'm such a wise guy."

Yes, Coop, you were our wise guy. If anything was going to happen, if an adventure or quest could be made, if someone could make an obstacle course out of anything, you were all in.

Shortly before he died, Cooper announced one day, "I'm bored. I need to build a box for my X-Box." And so he went to work. That boy could do absolutely anything when he set his mind to it. After he was finished, he proudly presented his beautiful, hand-crafted masterpiece. None of us knew at the time, how important this piece of wood molded by Cooper's own hands would become to our family. Sadly, we would soon find out.

ECCLESIASTES 3:4 (NLT)
"...a time to cry and a time to laugh.
A time to grieve and a time to dance."

CHAPTER TWENTY-THREE

The Donation

Cooper sustained a serious head injury at the end of his days on earth. It didn't take him from us immediately in body, but he had left us in mind.

When we gathered at the hospital, a nurse told us Cooper's case was grave, and asked us two questions. "Would you like a chaplain to visit? And do you want to see Cooper?"

Feeling numb and out of body, we nodded, "yes," to both. The chaplain came immediately and prayed with us as a family, then as a group, before we entered Cooper's room.

Amid the stark white walls, whirring machines, beeping monitors, and other things measuring and keeping Cooper's body physically alive, we stood. I looked at my husband and other children. Then I said, "Under the circumstances, what do you think about organ donation?"

We all agreed. Our Cooper would want it to give in his death as he'd done throughout his life. The nurse who'd stood discreetly at the back of the room said reverently, "I was going to bring it up. But absolutely, we can bring LifeSource in to talk with you."

LifeSource is a non-profit organization dedicated to saving lives through organ and tissue donation in the Upper Midwest. They serve over six million people in communities across Minnesota, North Dakota, South Dakota, and portions of Wisconsin. http://www.life-source.org

They are the federally-designated organization that manages organ and tissue donation in our region. They work with hospitals and community partners to support donor families and to facilitate the donation of organs and tissues to transplant recipients. They also encourage people to register as donors, something our family advocates as well.

Each region in the United States has a federally designated organization responsible for the oversight of compassionate transplant services, where living donors, donor families, and recipients are equally treated with concern. You can view national statistics broken out by region at this website: http://optn.transplant.hrsa.gov/converge/members/regions.asp. You can find the transplant agency for your state and region here: http://organdonor.gov/materialsresources/materialsopolist.html.

In our case, the LifeSource representative answered all of our questions, and filled in blanks for things we didn't know to ask. There was one thing in particular we needed them to tell us. "What will you do to Cooper?"

I admit to having dark thoughts when it came to gifting his tissue. Would they take my baby's skin? The thought made me shiver.

The rep soothed our concerns. "We treat your son as another living human being, no different than the recipient. He will receive the utmost care, dignity, and respect. His *life* is precious, not just his body parts."

LifeSource gave us comfort and made the choice easier, though we were pre-decided as a family anyway. Now it was up to Cooper to determine what parts of his body could renew life for others.

The doctors told us he was brain dead. When his vitals were taken, he measured 50 on the ventilator. If we made the choice to take Cooper off of life support, his organs would not be viable for transplant, we could only offer his tissues due to legal mandates.

To add to our excruciation, there was no way to predict how long Cooper's body would hang on after he was unplugged. It could be minutes, hours, days, or weeks.

Unsure and still unwilling to make that choice, we asked LifeSource if we could start the paperwork prior to knowing whether we would be able to give just his tissue, or if his organs would be included. They agreed, and we filled out the necessary documents.

The next evening, while my husband, our daughters, and I left to freshen up, Cooper's condition changed. Connor, our oldest and Coop's big brother, was alone when a nurse pulled him to the side and gently whispered, "He's no longer responding."

It was over.

We wanted to allow Cooper the chance to live on in others and offer more gifts of life through his organs as well as his tissues. And at the end, he did that — on his own terms.

His lungs went to a fifty-six-year-old. His pancreas to a sixty-one-year-old. Someone received Cooper's cornea and the gift of sight. Another man named Paul got a kidney and his liver. While the Paul whose story you're reading now, received the other kidney, and my sweet boy's generous and joyful heart.

It's fitting, since one of Cooper's best friends was named Paul.

After Cooper had given his final gifts, the hospital chaplain came to see us once again. "When the family is comfortable with it, we fly a Donate Life donor flag for all to see and honor those who sacrificed. Would you be willing for us to raise the flag on Cooper's behalf?"

"Of course," we all agreed. But Cooper's siblings wanted to take things a step further.

"Can we go through the ceremonial flag folding and raising ourselves? Every one of us has done it multiple years at youth camps, and we're very experienced. We want to do this for our brother."

The chaplain crinkled his eyebrows and said, "We've never been asked that question before." He tapped his finger against his lips. "I don't see why not."

And so, when the moment came, our three children stood beside the hospital's flag pole and solemnly gave tribute to our Cooper. The boy who had given us so much.

As the helicopter waited to leave with the last cooler housing Cooper's precious cargo, we stood united, tears streaming off our chins. The blades spun faster, flinging dust and small debris in a wide sweep around the bird's base. It swayed as it lifted off the ground. Hovering briefly while it gained altitude, then within seconds, it moved away from the building.

One of the kids shouted, "Go get 'em, Cooper."

Someone else added, "Give them your best."

Then another voice finished for us all, "Enjoy the ride."

With that, the helicopter flew out of sight. Cooper as we'd known him, would soon transform like a caterpillar into a butterfly, cocooned in other bodies — while his spirit soared, as free as the wind.

JOHN 15:13 (NLT)
*"There is no greater love than to lay
down one's life for one's friends."*

CHAPTER TWENTY-FOUR

Saying Goodbye

A parent should never have to experience it.

Standing in the urn room at the crematorium almost knocked me to my knees. It's the single hardest thing I've ever had to consider — which beautifully crafted piece would hold the priceless treasure — my son's ashes. All I could do was repeat, "My son doesn't belong in one of these. My son doesn't belong in there."

Today, I still say, "My son didn't belong in one of those."

We decided to have Cooper's body cremated, so we could keep a physical piece of him with us. We separated his ashes into four parts, one for each of his three siblings, and the remainder, placed in the beautiful wooden box crafted by his own hands for his X-Box game. Cooper didn't know it at the time, but his masterpiece was made for something much more special than a video console, it houses the part of his ashes for his dad and me.

Cooper gave us many gifts through every day life while he was with us on earth. But after his death, I believe he had one more surprise in store. Something special, a Coop Man kind of message.

Five years before Cooper died, he discovered a passion for tending tea roses. He planted red and white, the Monroe and Kennedy varieties, in our back yard. Fitting, since Marilyn and Jack died before their time too.

Cooper left us in March of 2014, a few short weeks before his roses would have bloomed, except something strange happened that year. His carefully cultivated flowers seemed to know the loss we were struggling to bear. They appeared to grieve with us.

As if to say, "We miss you too," neither of his tea roses blossomed in the late spring and early summer of 2014. Stubbornly, though the stems were green, because Cooper's hands no longer tended them, his roses did not bud. They looked as stark as my soul felt.

How I made it through that summer, I'm not really sure. How my other children and husband survived the deep darkness that swallowed up any sunshine, I do not know. Nothing made sense. Cooper's rose bushes symbolized what we couldn't ignore. They shared their thorns, but not their fragrance. Cooper's life once scented with all the things of life, now stung in the tragedy of his death.

Why Cooper's rose bushes stood flowerless after five straight years of producing velvet petals, we couldn't answer. But it was fitting. My son was no longer here to tend them. He was no longer here to tend to us.

Several months after Cooper's passing, in the autumn of 2014, I glanced out the window into my back yard. A curious sight caught my eye. What was it? Could it be? Was it possible?

I walked out the door, and made my way to Cooper's tea roses. Unexpected, out of season, a single white blossom boldly spread her petals, as if taking a final breath. Mesmerized I brushed her pure, soft folds.

I imagined Cooper slipping in during the night and coaxing his beloved rose to bloom one more time. My boy wanted us to know he was still producing life.

The essence of Cooper's sacrifice is bound in our family's love. And with every heartbeat that pulses in Paul's chest, we feel beauty in the broken places where Cooper is missing.

Though his spirit has moved on, we have the hope and confidence that Cooper is still with us. Through the many lives he saved, and through the tenderness of a message sent through a rose. Cooper continues to bloom, like a white rose in autumn daring to spread his spirit like petals drawing another breath. Our Cooper brightens the world, and we are blessed to know and share him. His color will never fade — he will not die. He has simply transformed.

Paul didn't know it, but after we laid Cooper to rest, I waited and waited to receive a letter from one of his recipients. I, too, was afraid of stirring up painful memories for those who had gotten one of my son's organs or tissues. But I desperately wanted to learn about them. Part of my child now abided in their bodies, and I felt drawn to find out who they are.

My family and I are so grateful Paul took the courageous step to write us a letter — not all do. But it's one more confirmation of Cooper's legacy. It's another piece of evidence that his spirit lives on. It's another velvet bloom, coloring the world with beauty, and reminding us, there is life after death.

We may not always understand why things happen on earth, but in Heaven all will be made clear. We trust it is there, we will see our boy again — Cooper whole, restored by God to his perfect self. We miss him, but we look forward to that day.

Cooper is still a force. In his death he is still giving life. We are proud to know him. Blessed to call him ours. Honored to give him to the recipients he saved. Happy to share his story with you. May Coop's sacrifice inspire you to do something special for someone else today — a mother could ask for no greater legacy for her child.

JONAH 2:7 (NIV)
"When my life was ebbing away, I remembered you, Lord, and my prayer rose to you, to your holy temple."

CHAPTER TWENTY-FIVE

Takeaway Lessons from my Doctors

Cooper's family made me feel as if my own family suddenly grew by five people. I hate the circumstances of our meeting, but I'm thankful we did.

I almost missed my transplant because of several different episodes, but apparently God isn't done with me yet. I believe He wants me to share many things from my personal experiences, and the diversity of people he sent that transformed my life.

By the time I was released for home in Missouri, I had a whole team of doctors — cardiologists, nephrologists, gastroenterologists, dermatologists, surgeons, physical therapists, and my primary care physician. Each one had unique perspectives, but there were also patterns in what they shared about my condition and healing in general — both from a patient's viewpoint, and from a caring advocate.

These questions were asked of each person interviewed during the research phase of this project. "If you were sitting across the table from the reader of this book, over lunch, coffee, tea, or a soda, what takeaway would you want them to receive? What personal insights would you like to share with them? What might they not know, that they do not realize they don't know?"

The responses were insightful.

My primary cardiologist, Dr. Jerry Dwyer, is not a tall man, I'd guess he's around 5'8". This is obvious when he stands next to my 6'4" frame. But when he's talking medicine and treating the human condition, he's a giant in stature. His patient care is always genuine.

Jerry's office represents his personality well. No-nonsense, practical, and orderly, but not compulsively so. Yet, there's a down to earth warmth about him, reflected in the blues, greens, and browns used in his favored color schemes — and his love of Diet Coke.

His method of communicating mirrors his other traits. Discussing my case, he clicked a can of Diet Coke open, took a sip, then revealed his thoughts.

"Paul is an inspiration, even to a realist like me. He defied the odds. Paul fought hard, even Paul doesn't know how sick he really was. He died at least twice, was resuscitated numerous times, sometimes while his chest was still open. Even for me it was strange to see his heart when it was no longer beating.

I have to tell you, we're more than patient/physician, I'd call Paul a friend, and it was hard seeing him struggle to live."

A knock sounded on the door, and a nurse peeked around the frame. "I'm sorry to interrupt, but there's a patient on the phone with a question."

He didn't hesitate to respond. Excusing himself with a quick apology, Dr. Dwyer promised to return. Then he left the room and took the call.

A few minutes later, Jerry returned. "Sorry about that. Now where were we?"

Dr. Dwyer answered his own question. "That's right. In 2011, he was crashing. His heart was being assisted by external pumping machines. He went into renal failure — that's his kidneys. His entire body was in shock; then, he went into septic shock from infection. He wasn't waking up. He was in the ICU part of November, all of December, until he was transferred to a long term rehab facility in mid-January."

Dr. Dwyer shifted in his chair uneasily. "Honestly, I was waiting for him to die. I thought I'd lose him prior to Thanksgiving. Then I was sure 2012 was going to be the end, but Paul miraculously pulled through. He really has defied death many times over. He's a man living on borrowed time."

The physician's Irish cheeks reddened, and he stifled a sniffle before continuing. "Honestly, the statistics for heart transplant are dismal, though they are constantly improving. Luckily for Paul, he had the financial resources — ability to leave work and home — to go to Rochester and stay for months at a time as he waited for a transplant at Mayo. No matter how a person arranges their healthcare, focusing on it as the highest priority can mean the difference between life and death."

When asked about reader takeaway, Dr. Dwyer responded, "When you can, make it personal with your physician. Develop something to bond or connect with, create a relationship if you can. It really will improve your healthcare if your medical team feels like they can partner with you to fight for your own good health.

Also, give to others. Supporting where you can — whether financially, emotionally, or spiritually, it really helps give patient's a sense of purpose. Advocating for causes and other people is a great way to invest yourself for your own good and that of others."

He took a thoughtful breath before continuing.

"Be brutally honest with your doctor — be clear in order

to help them make informed decisions on your behalf. When they need to be brutally honest with you, understand they are still human. They may try to hide it, but your life matters to them. If you sense that's not the case, it's time to look for a new physician."

Dr. Dwyer picked up a medical file.

"These documents prove the power of the human spirit. Paul refused to give up. Even with the best patient care, it still comes down to the desire to carry on. A patient's will to live can help them save their own life."

Jerry sighed.

"This one's hard but necessary for the sake of your loved ones. Come to terms with death. Decide how far you want your medical care to go. What will enable you to face death with dignity? Make sure you've expressed your desires to your family and closest friends. Put it in writing, so there is no question or argument as to your intent."

Suddenly, Dr. Jerry Dwyer's face took on an ornery grin.

"The last thing I'd say is, those three kids of Paul's better do good stuff. Every human being leads someone. Leadership is something to be taken seriously, and Paul has left a legacy of leadership to his children and community. They have an obligation to carry on in a manner fitting of their father and neighbor. Otherwise, what's the point in living?"

Great wisdom from a great man. Now you see why I appreciate him so much — as I do Dr. David Hayes.

When asked about reader takeaway, Dr. Hayes said this, "Mr. Perkins was in dire straights. His case brings a few things immediately to mind.

First, resiliency is necessary in a patient and their caregivers. The patient who comes in with a determination to maintain an optimistic attitude about their health has been shown to heal faster, as well as to enjoy a much higher quality of life.

Those who are pessimistic are prone to depression and

anxiety, which in turn can lead to greater physical health issues. Paul was told by other medical practitioners to give up, but Paul refused. He exercised that healthy balance between realism and optimism, exactly what was needed for him to beat the odds, and qualify for a transplant — thereby saving his life. He did not leave any stone unturned.

Part of resiliency is being your own advocate and proactively ensuring you are informed. Take the initiative. Say to yourself and those in the medical community, "I need to know what's going on so I can take optimal care of myself. If I don't get the answers I need, I will stand up for myself to get important information."

Dr. Hayes added a warning, "However, be careful about the intelligence you gather. Not everything on the Internet is credible."

The doctor ran a finger through his salty brown hair.

"Secondly, family and/or friend support is key. Gather help from others who are willing to learn with you and walk beside you."

Dr. Hayes took a moment to glance out of his office window, peering down to the bustling city street below, as if gathering his thoughts. In short order, he continued.

"Depression, anxiety, and post-traumatic stress are real enemies to healing. At least 50% of patients who believe they are losing mental battles will face greater physical symptoms as a result — some life-threatening.

Many healthcare institutions are not only acknowledging this reality now, but are approaching it with specified care targeting the mental health that goes hand in glove with physical health. If the physician doesn't open the door to this kind of conversation, the patient should. Talking about what's weighing on you actually helps lighten your emotional load."

Once again, Dr. Hayes deflected his attention temporarily toward the street-level activity below his office. A look of sadness crept over his kind features, before he tackled a tough point.

"When the prognosis is terminal — twenty-four months or less, there is a pattern people typically walk through. You can see the patient and their families cycle through the stages of grief. When this is the case, I personally believe it's important they study the Kubler-Ross method so they know what to expect, and can better understand what they're feeling. Most generally need help to walk through those necessary stages, so they can mourn and not get stuck.

I suggest to my patients with this prognosis, that they address things openly. Bring in palliative care, hospice, etc. Be willing to have an open discussion about end of life.

Sometimes the patient wants to have an open discussion, but the family doesn't. Sometimes it's the reverse — the family wants open discussion, but the patient doesn't. Either one of these scenarios can diminish the last chapter of their quality of life.

Go through a checklist of honest questions and answers regarding end of life. How do you want to spend your final days? In my book, *Understanding Your Pacemaker or Defibrillator: What Patients and Families Need to Know,* among other practical tips, I shared the N.E.E.D.S. acronym. It stands for:

Notify your loved ones of your wishes for end-of-life care related to your device, and document them legally.

Educate yourself about treatment options.

Evaluate all of your treatment options.

Discuss your preferences and consider palliative care.

Seek mental and spiritual health care to aid in this difficult time."

Dr. Hayes then offered my co-author a copy of his book,

one we both highly recommend. A peaceful smile spread to his cheeks.

"The last, and no less important suggestion I would offer your readers is to find something you can believe in. Something greater than yourself. Those who have a foundation of faith appear to do better, not just in surviving, but in experiencing a positive quality of life.

I've clearly seen the connection between mind, body, and spirit in bringing about whole health. If one of those elements is missing, statistically speaking, the patient just doesn't do as well."

Do you see a pattern emerging from among some of the greatest medical minds who cared for me? And Dr. Borgeson hasn't weighed in yet.

Each of my physicians have their own style, I simply do not have enough room to share the wisdom of Dr. MoDad, Dr. Mauney, Dr. Edwards, or any of the others not specifically outlined in this book. But there is one more physician whose detailed tactics could potentially save a person's life. In my humble opinion.

Dr. Borgeson's style is to provide concise information in a warm, yet powerful way. His tips for readers include the following:

1. If something doesn't make sense, look for answers.

2. Never forget, there is hope. There's always a chance.

3. If someone tells you there's a 99-1 chance you'll be dead within the year, ask yourself, "What do I have to do to be that one percent who isn't?"

4. Life absolutely is a marathon, so stop trying to sprint. Don't micro-analyze things. Exercise caution, but don't tear the life you have to shreds looking for something that isn't there. There will be days when you wonder if it's

all worth while. Don't question it. The answer is, "YES!"

5. Pay attention to long-term results so you can measure progress in a healthy way. If you only look at the day to day, you may be too close to get an accurate view. Ask yourself, *Am I, or the person I love who's ill, having more better days than two weeks ago?* If the answer is "yes," then you are probably on the right path. Or are there more difficult days than there were two weeks ago? If this answer is yes, then you need to look for alternative answers.

Dr. Borgeson was clear in what he communicated. He didn't shy away from hard truths.

He said, "You're going to hear a lot of things you don't want to hear as a cardiologist patient — but do your job.

I outline the patient's job this way:

1. Pay attention.

2. Watch.

3. Don't avoid. Tell your doctor honestly how you feel, then let them deal with the details.

4. Be an advocate for yourself (or the patient if you are not the one who is sick).

5. Understand the why behind what medications you take — this makes you much more likely to do good things for yourself.

6. Remember that it is a long term process.

7. Don't let things go too long.

8. Give yourself permission to get better.

9. Do not live out the definition of insanity — doing the same thing over and over, yet expecting a different result.

10. Continually ask yourself, *What can I do to be in that*

percentile that survives and thrives with an improved quality of life?

11. The doctor's job is to tell the patient what the options are, the patient's job is to choose.

12. Focus on the issue. Ask yourself, *What is the issue?* Don't allow distractors to throw you off course.

13. Don't allow fear of losing your doctor to stop you from furthering treatment. If someone/something else is suggested to take you to the next step, jump at the opportunity. A comfort zone is usually not a good place for a patient to sit in.

14. Know you need to grieve — and face each stage in the process. You'll often grieve mobility, good health, the ability to do things you used to enjoy.

15. Celebrate small victories.

He added a few more intriguing details for good measure.

"I find the men I treat live in denial and the women obsess. Together they become one complete human being. God wired women and men differently, and their care generally requires a different approach. This is why husband and wife teams help a physician balance their efforts.

Every human being needs something to push them forward. Have short term, intermediate, and long term goals. For instance, say things like this to yourself, *Today, I'm going to get out of bed and walk down the hallway four times."*

"This week, I'm getting out of the hospital."

"This year, I'm going on the vacation I've wanted to take."

Come to think of it, I wonder if he spoke my family to make them push me so hard. But knowing them, I doubt they required spurring.

Dr. Borgeson wasn't just all about facts though. One of the reasons I hold him in such high esteem is his willingness to show strength of mind, and how he touches the human spirit — even expressing his own vulnerability.

He said, "As a physician, it's the ones who don't survive that stick with you more. Paul's story is a survival tale, and it's nice to remember someone like him — because it's highly unusual."

In regard to my case, Dr. Borgeson said, "Paul can attest, when you are seriously ill, especially where transplants are involved, there will most likely be a time where you want to quit. Where you want to die, because you feel so bad. But if you stick it out, if you direct your thoughts to every optimistic hope you have, if you reach out to your support team, though everything in you says pull away, if you clutch your faith, then one day, you will get through this stretch. Your faith will be made sight.

Paul did not receive his transplant because he was wealthy. He got it because he was in the right place, at the right time, with the right illness, with the right mental makeup. In Paul's case, he knows there was a greater plan at work that threaded those elements together. Why? He can't answer. But I trust he will spend the rest of his life working to fulfill the purpose behind God's plan."

He concluded by saying, "We will all die — including your physician. Your doctor is not in control, they are not God. But we often have a choice in the quality of life until God calls us home."

I remain in awe of the physicians who cared for my body, while they stood as protectors of my mind and spirit. For me, it's evidence proving that God is real and willing to provide. After all, He is the Great Physician.

My family was also asked to answer the same questions for potential readers. Some of the things they shared brought tears to my eyes, even though their answers were given for the benefit of others.

MATTHEW 9:12 (NKJV)

When Jesus heard that, He said to them, "Those who are well have no need of a physician, but those who are sick."

CHAPTER TWENTY-SIX

Tribute to My Caregiver

All three of my children amaze me. We parents often feel disappointed in ourselves, focusing on all we did wrong, with little celebration of what we did right. My illness and subsequent deaths allowed me to see my children under pressure, and to see my parental successes, in spite of my fatherly failures.

This is why I'm so proud of what my kids have to offer you. When asked what they wanted readers to take away from this story, each in their own way, said they wanted those who read this book to know the lasting power and impact of simple family moments.

In particular, they each expressed their recognition and appreciation for their mom's daily giving. I couldn't agree more.

Scott said this of his childhood memories.

"No matter how tight things were, or how busy our schedules, Mom always made sure we ate a healthy, home-cooked meal. A full breakfast in the morning. Pancakes. Bacon. Eggs. Hot cereal. When we were home for lunch, grilled cheese and tomato soup, or some other nutritious fare. A hearty dinner in the evening. Often steak and potatoes, roast and vegetables, or carbohydrates if we needed them for a ball game that night. Sometimes she switched it up, and we had breakfast for supper, but we never missed a meal. Even when Dad worked late at the bank, Mom made sure we didn't wait or want. The things I took for granted while they were happening are the things that have impacted me the most."

Julie added.

"What I learned from Mom's example was to care for others in acts of loving service, and to give anonymously.

At Christmas, she gives each of her grandchildren a certain amount of money for them to spend on other people. She secretly gives to hard-working people, never letting others know, never wanting acknowledgment or attention.

Your legacy is the very last gift you leave the world. My mom multiplies hers with each undisclosed act of kindness she offers. She makes me want to touch others as she does, I want to be more like her every day."

Mark's sentiments were similar. "I don't remember eating out as a child, Mom fixed a full home-cooked meal and had it on the table every night. My favorite before games was honey and toast. Mom always made sure her family came first. As a parent, I want to be more like her."

Scott followed up.

"My parents rarely missed a school activity. I can't remember one time when I didn't hear dad cheering for every basket, or see Mom documenting every free throw. I'd look up in the stands to see the bulky, black RCA camcorder resting on Mom's shoulders as she waved it back and forth to capture my accomplishments, as well as my mishaps, on the court or field. Sometimes I worried she'd hit the person next to her and knock them down the bleachers in her excitement over a big play.

Thankfully, she never did.

Mom also made her own stat sheets for basketball and baseball, the two main sports I played. No pre-printed fill in the blanks statistical forms, she created her own hand printed charts where she could track every basket made, every shot missed, each hit leading to a double base run, or error allowing another runner to advance around the bases. She didn't miss a thing.

Mom was the detailer in the family. When we went on family vacations during my younger years, we typically drove, because we couldn't afford the money for all of us to get plane tickets. Mom would map out an itinerary for us, to the minute, ensuring our vacation was complete on paper, and allowing us to do everything we hoped for when we arrived.

Back in the day, Mom was the navigator while Dad drove. She'd highlight our route, follow it with her fingers, and provide turn by turn directions. Before they existed, Mom was the GPS of our family trips. She kept us on track -- most of the time.

There were only a few occasions where we got off course, and things got a little bumpy inside the car, as Dad and Mom debated over the best way to get back on track. But even then, it struck me that those tense moments didn't last long. My parents seemed committed to getting along.

When my brother, sister, and me were growing up, Dad was big, strong, and athletic. Mom was strong in her own way, she nurtured us, and made us feel secure.

My mom taught me grace, dignity, silent strength, and compassion for others -- especially from what I've watched her endure during Dad's illnesses. She planted a legacy in me as well."

My kids remind me that failure is often perceived. Children are resilient, and absorb more good than we sometimes realize.

Recently, for Linda's sixty-fifth birthday, the family gathered around and each person read a personal piece they'd written about her. In the face of overwhelming uncertainty, our family likely would have crumbled, had it not been for my wife.

Like the engraving on our wedding rings, she's still the strength hidden behind the band of our family unit. My wife's softness has protected our relationships through many trials. It isn't the harshness people see in our circumstances, but the softness of my wife, pressing against the hardness of adversity that has protected us all.

She continues to bless us with her endurance and example. Linda's wisdom is evident in all the other things my family exhibits.

PROVERBS 5:18 (NLT)
"Let your wife be a fountain of blessing for you.
Rejoice in the wife of your youth."

CHAPTER TWENTY-SEVEN

A Miracle Man's Wonderful Life

When we're young, death usually seems far away — a lifetime to be exact. In our youthful minds, history means nothing, after all, it's just boring stories about old people we didn't know. Doomed to repeat the mistakes of those who came before us? Never! We're too smart for that.

The arrogance of youth produces dangerous attitudes. When we face our own demise, we are shocked into reality. Without my wife, children, grandchildren, and close friends, I would not be alive today. They navigated, carried, and nudged me when it was necessary for my healing. But I give the highest thanks to God Almighty, who not only saved me physically, but renewed me spiritually. He gave me hope and restored me when I was ready to give up.

My hope isn't solely because I died two times and was resuscitated to live again. My joy isn't exclusively because I was given the rare opportunity to visit Heaven and to attend my own funeral, although those experiences transformed my understanding.

My excitement is the result of my deepened relationship with Jesus Christ now, while I'm still on earth. I am passionate to share my hope and joy, because I believe there are many like me, before God restored my life.

Sometimes we appreciate the most important things least, because they hide in plain sight beneath lifelong habits. That's why my priorities were wrong.

According to doctors I am a walking miracle. Yes, I defied death not once, but multiple times. But I am more than my miracle. I am a man who has been born again.

After experiencing death, I know my poverty of spirit while I chased worldly things, ignoring God's call. Today, I realize that I sacrificed precious time on the altar of immediate gratification.

I can't go back and do things over again, but I can choose more wisely now. In life I can make a fresh start. In death it will be too late.

Before my illness, my priorities were:

1. Family

2. Self

3. Friends

4. Career

5. God

Today, my priorities are:

1. God

2. Family

3. Friends

4. Others

5. Self

I honor God first, followed by the care of my family, and

invest in friendships. Next, I help others; then I refill myself. If I don't maintain my body, mind, and spirit, and if I don't love myself in a healthy way, I will have nothing to give to anyone.

While God was realigning my priorities, He opened my eyes to something else. Dramatic events woke me up, and I understood that God doesn't owe me a single thing. He doesn't owe me wealth, comfort, my house, my family, or my health. God certainly doesn't owe me eternity in Heaven.

I, however, owe Him everything. I owe Him a, "Yes," to His offer for a relationship with His son, Jesus Christ.

He is God. He is good. He is worth risking everything for.

Like Job, I enjoyed a comfortable life. Yet I discovered, everything was meaningless when the things I treasured most were no longer there.

I became the man who lived to play basketball, but could no longer shoot. The man who was excited to play in a golf tournament, but couldn't swing the club. I could no longer bathe or dress myself. I couldn't even get out of bed. I slid to the lowest place I could imagine.

From the time I was young, I thought I was made to teach and lead — I was wrong.

The humility of having everything stripped away showed me that I was really made to serve. To serve God and my fellow man.

The doctors cannot explain why I'm alive. But even more so, how I'm walking and talking. They call me a miracle man. I call myself a miracle man with a purpose.

Because of the longevity and complexity of my illness, because of what I saw and experienced in my deaths, because of God's love, grace, and power demonstrated in my life, I am committed to spreading the good news of His love and willingness to heal. Whether on earth or in Heaven.

For whatever time remains, I want to shout His praise, and lift the spirits of others.

If you or a loved one is facing a transplant, I trust you've gleaned practical, emotional, and spiritual insight. In some ways you trade one disease for another, from the aspect that every day requires careful planning to protect the new organs. However, a transplant can also extend life and substantially improve the quality of it.

If you have lost someone you loved, or if you are among the thousands who fear dying, I hope you find comfort in my story. Death is not the end. I can tell you, the best is yet to come — if you choose to believe.

If you are reading this book because you are concerned about the afterlife, know your last breath does not end it all. You are able to choose your eternal destination now. I pray you call out to Jesus, while you still have a voice. When you stop running and submit, the results are beyond imagination.

I've tasted God's goodness beyond the grave. He only gave me a few moments, but that was enough to satisfy my soul. I am still excited about Heaven when God calls me home.

George Bailey, a fictional character, was able to see his impact through a non-life experience — as if he'd never been born. I was allowed a peek into my impact after death — when I witnessed my own funeral.

A wonderful life is grounded in simple and spiritual foundations, basic tenants of hope, faith, and love. These are available to everyone. Including you.

I've met people who want to know what happens when they die. Many ask me about Heaven. Some dare to question, "Are Hell and Heaven real?"

With blushed cheeks, some have asked, "Does God exist?"

These are all important questions, and I am grateful I can offer assurances that God and Heaven are real. Through faith and experience, I am confident that when you accept Jesus' invitation to a committed relationship with Him, Hell will no longer be your destination.

But there's something equally important right here, right now. Please don't miss this crucial understanding.

We get one shot at life on earth, and we are supposed to do something meaningful with it. Something that honors God and his son, Jesus Christ. Something inspired by the Holy Spirit. Something that serves our fellow man. We are meant to fulfill a purpose greater than ourselves.

What is it?

That's a question I can't answer — it's between you and God. I encourage you to actively begin your quest. Seek God until He reveals it. (Jeremiah 33:3)

Do your part. Go out into all the world and make a difference. Start small and build your way up.

You are meant for more — grab it while you can. Then when you see Heaven with your own eyes, you will hear God say, "Well done, good and faithful servant! You have been faithful with a few things; I will put you in charge of many things. Come and share your master's happiness!" (Matt. 25:23 NIV)

HEBREWS 2:4 (HCSB)
"At the same time, God also testified by signs and wonders, various miracles, and distributions of gifts from the Holy Spirit according to His will."

Epilogue

My hands felt a bit shaky on the steering wheel — part thrill, part nerves. Autumn leaves in yellow, crimson, orange, and brown fluttered to the ground as I pulled the car into their driveway. Linda and I opened our doors and got out. I exhaled loudly, true to my nature, while my wife appeared calm. I knew, however, beneath the surface her nerves were as rattled as my own.

We walked to the front door together. I knocked, wondering about the emotions of the people on the other side.

Robin and Tony McKinnon, my donor Cooper's parents, welcomed us inside. We had met with their daughter, Devin, several weeks before when she visited Missouri. But this was our first interaction with her mom and dad. Based on the reason for our meeting, we were all apprehensive — although a miscommunication about dates had allowed me to talk with Robin on the phone the day before.

I looked at my cell and saw Robin's name. "Hello."

Even though it was the first time I'd heard her voice, her stressed emotions were evident. "Are you okay?"

"Yes. Why?"

"I thought you were coming at 1:00."

Panic rose from my stomach to my chest. "I thought we were meeting tomorrow."

Robin released a loud breath. "I am so sorry. I guess I got the dates wrong."

We both chuckled nervously, and Robin said, "Now I have to try and look pretty two days in a row."

That made me laugh harder. "If that's your only complaint, we're off to a good start. I'll see you tomorrow. Okay?"

"I'll be ready. Again." Robin was chortling when we ended the call.

Now, as my wife and I stood in front of Cooper's parents, none of us laughed during our initial introductions. We needed to break the ice.

Robin and Tony offered us refreshments as we sat down. They asked Linda and me about ourselves. My wife told them about our children and grandkids, and I talked about our businesses. I didn't think I should focus on my health issues right away. But soon, the subject did arise, which led to discussing Cooper's life.

Robin shared a couple of Cooper's stories, reducing our anxiety. She asked, "Would you like to see some family photos?"

"Sure," Linda and I said eagerly.

Our fears left as Cooper's proud parents shared graduation photos, family portraits, and silly poses with friends. There was even a shot with Cooper clowning around wearing a purse on his arm, and we all laughed together.

It didn't take long for us to feel like we were in the company of friends.

A sense of humor and comforting words changed the way we felt. Mourning with them, showing compassion and empathy, instead of pity, made all the difference. In that one day, we experienced many emotions with Cooper's family.

After we finished looking at all of the photos, Robin told us about Cooper's Donate Life flag, and asked if we would like to see it as well. We nodded enthusiastically.

When Cooper's older brother, Connor, came in, he snapped a picture of the four of us, his parents with Linda and me, holding Coop's Donate Life flag. Capturing that moment sealed the bond between all of us.

Before we left that first day, I told Tony and Robin our plans to set up a Cooper McKinnon memorial fund in honor of their son's life and their family's brave sacrifice. We were all on the verge of tears.

"We want to spread the word about organ donation, create a lasting legacy for Cooper, and help improve the lives of others," I told them. Then we exchanged quick hugs. We would return and visit them again, before we left for home the next day.

The next morning, we stopped for a last goodbye with the McKinnons on our way to the airport. My voice choked as I considered their loss. And I realized, in many ways, they were my new extended family.

At the door, we embraced. I offered a promise. "You'll always have a broken piece in your heart, but you'll always know where it's at. Cooper's heart beats in my chest for you."

I am here because of courageous love. However many days God deems for me to continue, I will honor my gift of life. For Cooper. For our families. For friends. For my medical teams. For strangers. For Christ.

By God's grace, I defied death, and he redefined my life through the adversities I experienced. I realize now that beyond this moment, none of us are promised another day. I ask myself a series of questions on a regular basis.

If you knew this was your last breath, where would you go?
What would you do?
Who would you hug, kiss, and say, "I love you," to?
What appreciation would you express?

Then I say to myself, *No excuses — do it now. You won't be sorry if you do, but you might be sorry if you don't.* I also learned my miracle was not for me to hoard.

I exist not for myself, but for a greater good. This is the essence of a life lived in the shadow of God's grace and mercy. I am defined not by my mistakes, not by my accomplishments, but by a love that will carry me into eternity — my mission is to let others know they can have it too, simply by asking. On earth or in Heaven, because of Christ in me, it's a wonderful life.

Paul and Linda's Wedding Day

*A young Paul and Linda with Paul's parents, Tick
and Lucille at graduation.*

Scott, Julie, and Mark Perkins

Paul and Linda with all the Grands

Yadi in Minnesota snow

Alex and Julie Settles

Paul and Linda today

Cooper with Black Beauty

Cooper and friends

Cooper and his loves

Cooper, Robin, and Tony McKinnon

Cooper's Donate Life flag with his parents
and Paul and Linda

A future better than you imagined

Paul Perkins

Paul Perkins inspires audiences in churches and organizations around the country with his uplifting message, "Never give up." He speaks from a place of experience after years of battling chronic illness, undergoing a double transplant for his heart and kidney at the Mayo Clinic in Rochester, Minnesota, sparring with death multiple times, and even glimpsing the after-life.

For over 50 years, Paul has influenced the banking industry through his work and leadership at First Community National Bank. However, after his relationship with Jesus Christ, his greatest accomplishment is his family. Married to his bride of forty-six years, Linda, they are the proud parents of three children, Mark, Scott, and Julie, who have given them nine amazing grandchildren.

After God, family, and country, Paul's greatest passions include breathing in the beauty of the outdoors, especially when he's farming in Missouri, playing sports, he's determined not to let golf master him, and helping other people. For updates about Paul's ongoing journey, visit his Facebook page, Death Defied Life Defined.

Anita Brooks

Anita Brooks, is an award-winning author of multiple books. Her most recent, *Getting Through What You Can't Get Over,* (Barbour Publishing, 2015), won a Reader's Favorite International Book Award.

As an international speaker, and inspirational business/life coach, Anita motivates others to dynamic break-throughs. Blending mind, heart, body, and spirit, she shares hope and encouragement from the page and the stage — reminding audiences, "It's never too late for a fresh start with fresh faith."

Anita is also a living donor, honored to have given the gift of life in May, 1997, through a kidney transplant for her sister. Together, they are one of the longest surviving donor/recipient matches to date. Because of her experience, Anita works as a patient and donor advocate, advising medical teams and transplant agencies from a patient perspective. This is one way Anita fulfills her mission to help others transform life's battles into lasting victories. She has discovered purpose through her pain.

When she takes a break from speaking, coaching, and writing, Anita slips away to a lake or river with her husband of thirty-three years, Ricky. Their favorite pastime is watching sunsets, he while dipping his fishing pole in the water, she while dipping her toes.

Learn more at anitabrooks.com